401 R/C TECH TIPS

For your R/C Car.

by JIM NEWMAN

EDITOR'S INTRODUCTION

B uilding and racing R/C cars and trucks have evolved into an "immense" hobby that, for the dedicated enthusiast, requires myriad skills. It may be overwhelming at first, but, as you gain experience, the skills you acquire will bring you closer to being confident that you can deal with any challenge.

A knowledge of building, maintenance, tuning, driving and clean-up methods comes from reading instruction manuals, magazines, talking with others involved in the hobby, or simply by studying a problem and arriving at your own solution.

Starting with our first issue, *Radio Control Car Action* has included a monthly column called "Pit Tips." It features the best tips submitted by our readers. Produced by author and artist Jim Newman, "Pit Tips" is one of the most popular sections of the magazine, because each month, R/C enthusiasts find solutions to the simple, yet annoying, problems they face.

"Pit Tips" has covered a wide range of topics: motors, maintenance, suspension, chassis tuning, battery charging, tires and wheels, painting and detailing, radio gear, speed controllers and more. To find the solution to a specific problem, however, you just had to hope you'd find it in a particular issue. Now, with this "401 R/C Tech Tips" book, we've changed all that! We've compiled and categorized five years of "Pit Tips" into a volume in which you'll find the solution to your problems at the flip of a page.

STEVE POND

TABLE OF CONTENTS

Published by Air Age, Inc.
251 Danbury Road Wilton, CT 06897

—Manufactured in the United States of America—

Publisher: Louis V. DeFrancesco, Jr. Book Design: Alan J. Palermo. Art Production: Stephanie L. Warzecha. Art Assistance: Allyson Nickowitz. Editor: Steve Pond. Managing Editor: Li Agen. Copy Director: Lynne Sewell. Copy Editors: Katherine Tolliver and Brenda J. Casey. Assistant Copy Editor: Laura M. Kidder.

Illustrations by Jim Newman.

RADIO GEAR

The proper installation and maintenance of radio gear are extremely important to ensure correct operation for a long time. Here's a variety of tips to keep your radio and racing efforts on the same wavelength.

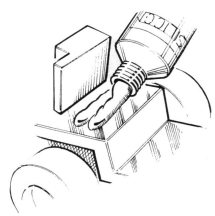

BETTER SERVO MOUNTING

When mounting your receiver and servos, etc., you'll find that double-sided adhesive tape has its limitations. Instead, you can set them in a thick layer of silicone rubber sealant. This holds firmly, yet it peels away without leaving any sticky residue when you need to remove the components.

QUICK CRYSTAL ACCESS

During a race, it's sometimes necessary to change frequency. If you own a Fox, this can be time-consuming because its chassis is sealed and dust-proof. Drill a 1/2-inch access hole over the crystal socket. Use needle-nose pliers on the plastic tab (not on the crystal's case) to extract the crystal, and after fitting the replacement, cover the hole with a piece of vinyl adhesive tape.

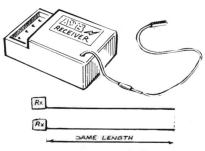

DETACHABLE ANTENNA

If you have two cars but only one receiver, you probably swap it from car to car. To avoid wearing the antenna wire by constantly wrapping and unwrapping it, cut the wire and solder in a small plug and socket. Each car can now have its own antenna permanently installed; merely plug it into the receiver. Be sure that the antenna stays at its original length before cutting, or you'll ruin the receiver's tuning.

TIDY ANTENNA

If you have a rigid, anti-roll-over-type "antenna" on your car, you can coil the receiver antenna wire around it as shown, then encapsulate it in heat-shrink tube for that neat-and-tidy look.

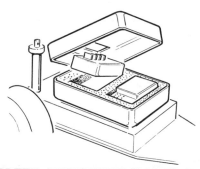

WATER-RESISTANT RADIO BOX

Fill a plastic soap box with sponge rubber; cut recesses for your receiver and battery; and lead the wires out through caulked holes. Then secure the box to the top of you car's original servo box with screws or double-sided tape, and hold the lid in place with rubber bands. Some speed controllers require a stream of cooling air, and for these, you'll need an opening in the lid and a sponge gasket as a seal against the top of the controller.

1 RADIO GEAR

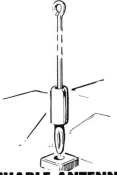

DETACHABLE ANTENNA

It's sometimes difficult to transport your car in a case without bending the wire antenna rod. Try this! Solder the antenna rod into a Radio Shack banana plug, then mount the socket on the side deck of your car. To travel, just unplug the antenna, but don't leave home without it!

STABILIZE YOUR SERVO

Check your steering servo; you might find it floats excessively on its rubber bushings and gives imprecise steering. The solution? Build up layers of double-sided adhesive tape so that the servo case sticks to the chassis platform. Clean the case with rubbing alcohol before you attach the tape.

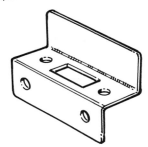

BLACKFOOT SWITCH BRACKET

This brass-sheet bracket replaces a broken BEC switch bracket. You can find inexpensive .032-inch brass sheet in the K&S Metal Center of your hobby shop. Cut the sheet to size, bend it over a hardwood block, then drill, cut and file the holes to fit the switch. Note that the switch guard is raised on one side.

OFF-ROAD INSURANCE

Off-road running will obviously have an adverse effect on your car. Why not waterproof the receiver, the battery pack and the speed controller by sealing them in thin plastic bags? Note how the ends of the bags are firmly bound with small rubber bands, or even cord, so that water doesn't seep down along the wires.

RECEIVER MOUNTING

Radio receivers can be conveniently mounted using Velcro®. Obtainable from any fabric store, it comes with a self-adhesive back, so it's ready to be used for installing components in the receiver and chassis. Changing receivers takes only a quick pull.

ANTENNA SHORTENING

Do *not* coil your antenna to shorten it, or you'll drastically reduce its range. This simple method is much better. Cut a piece of corrugated card that will fit into your car, then weave the excess antenna wire through alternate flutes or channels in the card.

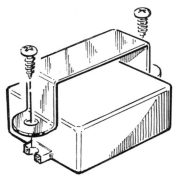

SERVO-CASE FIX

A broken mounting lug on a servo case led to this neat fix. You can use a piece of wire with a loop on each end, but the drawing shows a metal strap that's easy to make out of thin aluminum or tin-can stock. A thin piece of sponge rubber between the case and the strap should keep it snug.

SERVO-REVERSING

If you have an older Futaba Attack radio (the one without servo-reversing) and you need to "reverse" a servo, try this. Remove the transmitter faceplate, rotate the appropriate stick assembly 180 degrees (one half turn), then replace the plate. The stick action is now reversed so that you have the effect of a reversed servo.

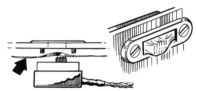

SWITCH SEAL

To avoid letting water and dirt enter through the switch opening and contaminate the contacts, cut a piece out of a thin plastic bag, remove the switch, then sandwich the plastic between the switch and the body. You could also use a piece of balloon rubber in this way, too; both work well.

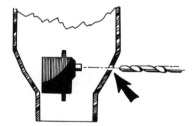

RC10 SERVO-ARM ACCESS

Here's a quick way to access the servo-arm retaining screw: carefully mark and drill a suitable hole in the side of the aluminum tub. The hole should be just large enough to accept a screwdriver. Now you can remove the servo arm without first removing the servo.

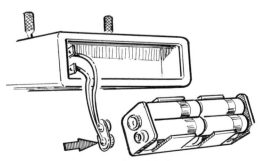

INTERMITTENT TRANSMITTER

Sometimes, we have trouble with intermittent battery contacts at the tabs inside the transmitter. To solve this, buy a Radio Shack no. 270-325 9V battery snap and solder its leads to the tabs; then snap the connector to your battery pack. You'll have no more problems.

EASY ANTENNA INSERTION

Before trying to slip the antenna wire up through the plastic tube, insert the spray tube of a WD-40 can into the tube, and give a quick squirt. Your antenna wire will slide through the tube surprisingly easily. (The WD-40 will quickly dry out.)

DESENSITIZE STEERING

Tackle the problem of over-controlled steering at the controller end of things. Wrap adhesive tape around the two sticks, then force ballpoint-pen tops over them to make them much longer. By doing this, you'll effectively "gear down" your control-stick movements.

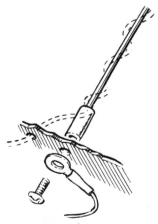

FOX ANTENNA MODIFICATION

After rolling your car a few times, you might notice that the insulation on its antenna is scratched and unsightly. Put the wire below the body shell, solder a lug to it, then clamp it to the screw under the rod base, thus making the wire rod the antenna. Be sure to range-check the radio with the motor running to see that you still have an adequate radio range.

1 RADIO GEAR

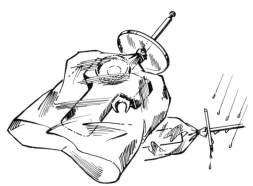

TRANSMITTER RAIN MITT

If you insist on racing in the rain, here's how to keep water out of your transmitter and prevent short circuits. Cover the unit with a large plastic bag, keeping the bottom open to allow your hands to enter. Securely tape the top end of the bag around the antenna, then punch a small hole in a plastic butter-tub lid and force this down over the antenna as far as the bag. The lid will shed any water that runs back down the antenna rod.

SHORTENED ANTENNA WIRE

Neatly stow that excess antenna wire! Cut this "comb" out of plastic or thin plywood, then zigzag the antenna wire through the slots. This device can be taped in a convenient place.

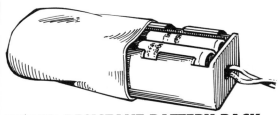

WATER-RESISTANT BATTERY PACK

This is a speedy way to make your battery box water-resistant. Simply cut an appropriate length of bicycle inner tube and slip it over the battery pack.

ANTENNA FISHING

Do you spend much time on trying to thread your antenna wire up inside the plastic hollow mast? Try this: suck a thread up through the tube, tie the wire to it and pull it through! Note the little barb cut into the antenna's insulation to prevent the thread from sliding off. You could also use CA to glue fine florists' wire into the end of the antenna wire, then push that up through the mast first.

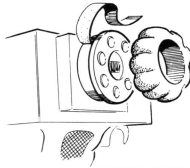

LOOSE CONTROLLER GRIP

If you see that the knurled grip is coming loose from the hub of your controller, as a quick trackside fix, you can increase the diameter of the hub slightly by winding a few turns of masking or electrical tape around it before you press the grip back on.

LOST ANTENNA BUTTON

If you've ever lost that little knob off the end of your antenna, then you'll know how difficult—if not impossible—it can be to raise the antenna. A replacement tip button is easily fitted by using a model plane wheel collar that fits the rod's diameter. If the antenna is hollow at its tip, slip a short length of wire inside it before you tighten the collar screw.

LOOSE SERVO CURE

If your servo sometimes wiggles, wedge a block of foam or cork between the servo and the chassis side member. It does the trick.

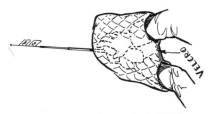

CONTROLLER MITT

If you race in cold weather, your freezing fingers will be insensitive, so why not make yourself a mitt that covers the controller and allows only the antenna to poke through. (Use an old towel or an old quilted jacket.) Your hands go through openings in the bottom and are away from winter's icy blast. Don't worry about not being able to see your hands. Do you ever look at your fingers while you're racing?

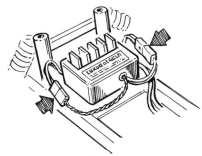

QUICK-CHANGE SPEED CONTROLLER

If you don't have enough electronic speed controllers for all your cars, solve the problem by cutting your controller's leads, inserting the appropriate plugs and sockets, and mounting the controller with Velcro®. You'll be able to move your controllers quickly from one car to another (and your receivers, too!).

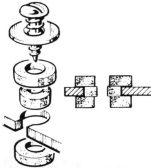

SIMPLE SERVO GROMMETS

Lost the rubber grommets for your servos? Two slices of surgical-rubber fuel line make excellent substitutes. Don't omit the smaller center slices; if the screws touch the servo flanges, they'll transmit vibration regardless of the presence of the remaining slices.

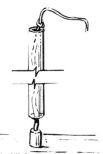

FLEXIBLE ANTENNA ROD

Some people dislike wire antenna rods because they have to straighten them—frequently! Replace yours with a plastic drinking straw. The straw plugs firmly over the original antenna mount, and your antenna wire now runs up through the middle and out of the top. Don't shorten the wire or double it back, or short range will surely result.

BLACKFOOT SERVO ACCESS

This simplified diagram shows a speedier method of accessing a Blackfoot/Monster Beetle servo and speed controller. Remove the heads from three screws, cross-drill for body clips, then screw into the cover as shown.

OPEN GIMBAL SHIELD

Open gimbal transmitter sticks quickly accumulate grass, dirt, etc. Cut foam-rubber dust excluders out of soft foam rubber.

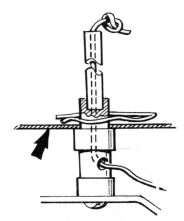

HOLE-SAVER ANTENNA MOUNT

This works with Parma's universal body mounts (it might work with others, too), and it's a way in which you can avoid having an additional hole through the body for the antenna. Simply drill a hole in the side of the mounting post, then plug the antenna tube into the hole in the top of the post, where it will fit perfectly. Now thread the antenna wire into the side hole and push it up through the tube, securing it at the top with a rubber band. (Arrow indicates the body.)

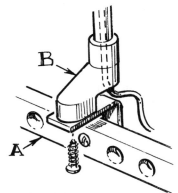

IMPROVED BLACKFOOT ANTENNA MOUNT

Do you want to eliminate the need to re-thread the antenna wire each time you remove the body shell? Attach a 1/2x1-inch aluminum (or, better yet, steel) bracket to the body-mount cross-brace, and then attach a chassis antenna-mounting bracket as shown. Enlarge the hole in the body to make it fit over the new bracket.

1 RADIO GEAR

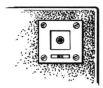

SERVO-REVERSING

An R/Cer who uses an inexpensive two-stick transmitter to control his cars doesn't have to mess with switching servo wires if servo-reversing becomes necessary. Instead, he can remove the four screws from the appropriate transmitter-stick assembly and rotate the entire stick 180 degrees before he replaces them. (Note the position of the trim levers in the drawings.) Certain radios might have screws inside them; if so, remove the back of the radio to reach to them.

TRANSMITTER STOPWATCH

Stick an inexpensive digital stopwatch onto your transmitter case, and use it for lap timing or recording battery time—important with a BEC.

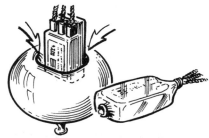

PROTECTION FOR ELECTRICS

To prevent water from getting into your receiver and speed controller, encase them in cut-up balloons, tying the rubber tightly around the wires, e.g., with rubber bands. You could also envelope your receiver in a partly inflated balloon, pressing the receiver into it as shown (so that it's in the center of the balloon donut). Then carefully release the air.

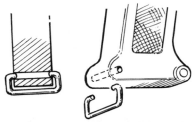

AIRTRONICS PISTOL-GRIP FIX

Has the strap holder on your pistol-grip radio broken off? Drill a hole through the radio's handle, and make a simple C-clip with ever-useful coat-hanger wire! Insert the clip's ends into the holes, and thread the strap through it.

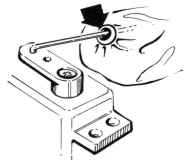

PUSHROD PROTECTION

If you protect your speed controller by putting it into a rubber bag, the bag might drag on the pushrod. To avoid this, put a shoe-lace grommet in the opening (shown by the arrow).

TIDY SERVO LEADS

To avoid having servo leads festooned across your car, you could tightly wrap each one around a suitable dowel, then remove the dowels and leave each lead neatly coiled. The inside of your car will look organized!

BATTERY CONNECTIONS

Each time you remove your battery, does the receiver battery holder fall out and put a strain on the wires until, eventually, they break? To solve this problem, buy a Radio Shack battery holder with the 9V-style snap-on connector, and attach a 9V snap connector to your battery leads. You'll be able to unsnap and remove the battery case for safe keeping.

CHAPTER 2

Their motors are the "hearts" of R/C cars and trucks. Properly maintained, they can provide months of useful service, but neglect is their worst enemy. The motor tips in this section should help keep your motor on the track for as long as possible.

MOTORS

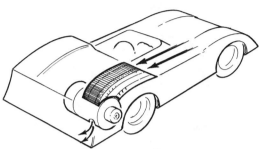

COOLING DUCT

Here's something you can do to lengthen the life of your brushes and commutator—blast cold air directly onto them. The duct is easy to make with an index card and tape. Cut an intake in your car's body (preferably in the scale position), and hold the duct in with dabs of bathtub sealant. It works! You might also get longer runs.

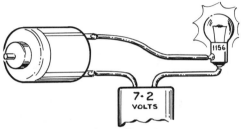

VOLTAGE DROPPER

Use the no. 1156 automobile light bulb that's often used for discharging battery packs. With a system of leads and crocodile clips or plugs, you can put this bulb in circuit (series) and use your stock 7.2V Ni-Cd pack to break-in your motor at a lower voltage: lower rpm without the expense of buying flashlight D-cells.

SOLDERLESS CONNECTIONS

Instead of soldering leads to motors, why not use crimped, solderless connections everywhere on your cars? To a short piece of connecting wire, crimp an eye-type terminal lug with a male plug-in terminal at the opposite end. The eye-type goes under the screws holding the motor-brush leads. Naturally, the female connectors fit on the leads into which the motor leads plug. You might have to snip one edge off the eye lugs to make room next to the bearing housing. Caution! When you're using crimped connectors, you *must* put *female* connectors on all *live* leads, e.g., the battery leads and controller leads, so that the live connections will be inside the insulating plastic sleeve. Connectors for crimping pliers are inexpensive and are sold at hardware stores.

COMMUTATOR CLEANER

Measure your commutator brushes, then cut a piece of the same size from a regular ink eraser. Push this into the brush housing until it bears firmly against the commutator. Rotate the armature until the commutator is brightly polished. Cut a piece off the pencil end of the eraser, and use it for a final burnishing of the copper segments.

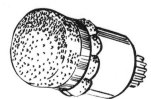

ENDBELL AIR FILTER

Here's another way of allowing cooling air to reach the commutator while keeping out grit. Hold a piece of thin, porous, foam plastic (of the bath-mat variety) in place with rubber bands or a piece of heat-shrink tube. It will completely cover the brush gear yet allow an air flow.

DUST FILTER

Need a filter? Take two used foam fabric-softener sheets, roll them around your motor, and staple them closed along the edge and across the ends, leaving the wires protruding. The sheets keep out dust and allow the engine to receive cooling air.

2 MOTORS

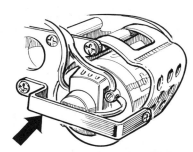

BRUSH-HOLDER GUARD

When the brush holder of this Optima took a solid hit that resulted in a "meltdown," its owner noticed that the regular motor guard hadn't protected that vital component. Make a protective extension with a strip of 1/8x1/4x3-inch steel.

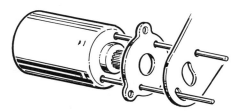

OPTIMA SPACER GUIDES

To keep parts aligned while you screw them together, insert two lengths of wire into the screw holes of the motor case, then through the spacer and into the motor-mount holes. Bring all three components together, withdraw one wire and insert a screw, then withdraw the second wire to insert the remaining screw.

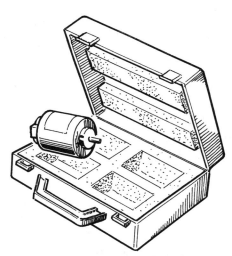

SPARE-MOTOR CARE

Spare motors should be treated kindly. Why not "nest" them in their own carrying case, e.g., an inexpensive plastic pencil box with snap latches. Line it with ordinary foam rubber, cut out nests for your motors, and glue foam retaining strips into the lid. The cost?—about $2.

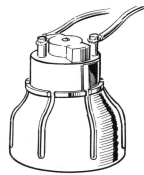

MOTOR-HOLDING JIG

This useful item can be found in almost any hardware store: a child-proof doorknob. Hot-glued to the end of your workbench or to a piece of wood, it holds a motor while you solder the wires into place.

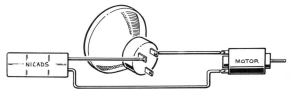

BREAKING-IN HIGH-POWERED MOTORS

No. 1156 bulbs only work on 540 motors, because they won't pass enough current to allow high-power motors even to turn over. A no. 6006 sealed-beam, 6V headlight is very reliable and costs about $5. Solder the wires straight to the two upper tabs (as shown), and you'll find that your motor runs at about the same speed as it would on two D-cells.

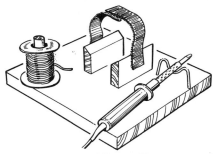

MOTOR SOLDERING JIG

This simple wooden jig not only holds the motor between the blocks with Velcro® while you're soldering, but it also holds the solder on a dowel spindle, and it has a simple wire rest for the iron. Drill holes in the wood so that the dowel and the wire rest can be glued into place. The device shown here measures 9x9 inches, and the spindle was made of a 1/2-inch dowel.

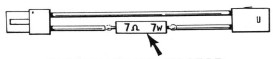

MOTOR BREAK-IN LEAD

By using a resistor in this adapter lead, you can use an existing 6-cell battery pack to break-in your new motor. The resistor drops the voltage to a sufficiently low level and, for a 6-cell pack, use a 7-ohm, 7W resistor from Radio Shack. *Caution:* use silicone-covered wire because the resistor gets *hot* when it's discharging.

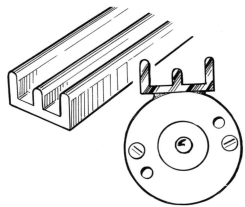

HOMEMADE HEAT SINK

The aluminum upper guides used on sliding doors make a fine heat sink when they're cut to length and glued to a motor. You could use CA to glue the rail to the motor case, but aluminum-filled epoxy might work better. You could also try curving the base of the sink so that it provides more contact with the motor case. Two or three sinks would get rid of the heat more efficiently than just one.

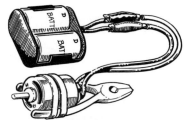

MOTOR BREAK-IN RIG

Here's a very inexpensive break-in rig: a Radio Shack D-cell battery holder (no. 270-386), two D-size batteries, two insulated battery clips. Total cost: approximately $3.85. The battery holder comes already wired, so just solder red and black alligator clips to the wires, "rubber-band" the motor between the handles of a pair of pliers, hook the leads to the motor wires, and away you go!

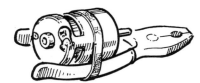

HOLD YOUR MOTORS

To stabilize your motors while you work on them, "nest" them between a pliers' plastic grips.

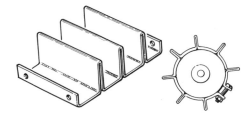

HOMEMADE HEAT SINKS

Fold thin aluminum sheet as shown. Using High-Temp Permatex, glue together the double layers that form the fins. When all has set, wrap the heat sink around your motor and secure it with two screws and nuts. (Put a tiny drop of thread-locking compound onto the threads.)

MOTOR-BEARING DIRT SEAL

The rubber shock gasket that usually fits over Tamiya's yellow shock units also snaps over the endbell bearing to keep dirt out and oil in. This simplifies maintenance and prolongs bearing life. Don't, however, use the gasket as an oil reservoir: too much oil passing through it will contaminate the commutator and damage the motor.

ENDBELL ALIGNMENT

Here's a clever way to make sure your endbell isn't fitted back-to-front. Before you remove it, use a sharp, pointed tool and a straightedge to scratch a line across the edge of both the endbell and the motor can. When you reassemble the motor, simply align the marks!

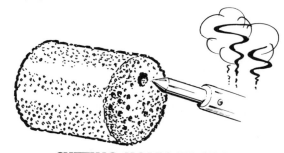

CUTTING HOLES IN FOAM

If you put foam dust covers over your motors, here's a way to cut neat holes for the motor wiring: simply use a pencil-type soldering iron to make a hole in the foam.

MOTOR HOLDER

Save an old tire or two, and use one to hold your motor vertical while you work on it.

CHAPTER 3

SPEED CONTROLLERS

Speed controllers can be a most confusing topic for beginning and experienced modelers alike. These tips tell you about them and their proper use and maintenance.

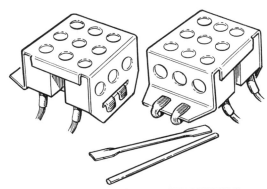

HEAT-SINK RETAINERS
If you lose the fiberboard retainer, and your porcelain heat-sink elements fall out, try this quick fix. Cut two 1 1/2-inch lengths of solder, flatten the ends, slide one end into the slots, then bend the tabs down. Now bend the other ends around the flange, and crimp them tightly with pliers to get your car back in business.

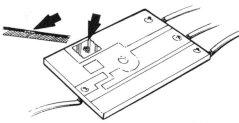

CONTROLLER BURNOUT
Here's the copper foil on a Super Shot controller; see how arcing (or sparking) has burnt a hole in it? The remedy? Put a spot of slow-setting CA into the hole, and then quickly cover it with cellophane adhesive tape until it has cured. When you remove the tape, polish the spot with something like no. 600 emery paper, and your controller should function properly.

SPEED-CONTROLLER COOLING
There's a raised lip on the roof of the Optima, and to increase cooling, you can cut out the front of this lip to form an air scoop. Glue in a plastic deflector to direct the airflow downward onto the unit.

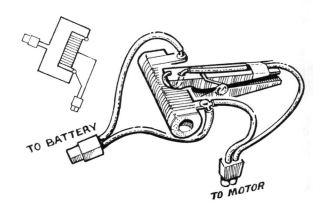

BENCH SPEED CONTROLLER
This item is useful when you're testing, cleaning and breaking-in motors. Its essential components are an unused speed-controller resistor and a clothespin. Drill the end of the pin as shown, feed the wire through the hole, and secure it with a drop of glue. Connect everything as shown, and attach the required plugs.

CONTROLLER CLEAN-UP

To clean the track of your speed controller, simply use a pencil eraser to make it bright and shiny.

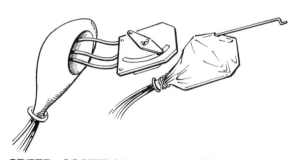

SPEED-CONTROLLER DIRT EXCLUDER

Cut a small opening in the side of a balloon, then feed the speed controller's wires into it so that they emerge through its neck. Now you can stretch the balloon loosely over the speed controller and let the pushrod come through a small hole to the servo.

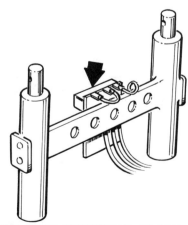

BLACKFOOT RESISTOR MOUNTING

If your car's front wheels splash mud and water onto your speed-controller resistor, move the controller to the rear of the body-post bracket and attach it with J&B Weld silicone glue. This will keep the unit high and dry and reduce the risk of breakage caused by thermal shock.

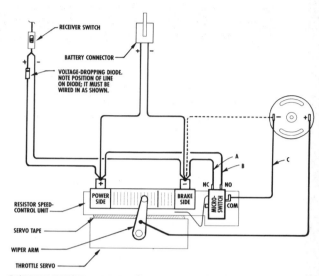

SIMPLIFIED PARMA RESISTOR DIAGRAM

Here's a less confusing diagram for the Parma variable-speed resistor unit. It provides for reverse, but to eliminate this feature, you should omit the microswitch and wires A, B and C, and make only the connection shown by the dotted line.

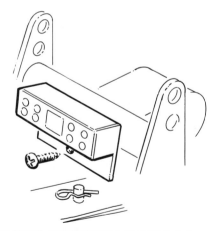

FALCON RESISTOR DAMAGE

To protect the resistor on your a Falcon, mount it between the shock towers in place of the receiver batteries, because with BEC, the batteries aren't necessary. To cool the resistor more effectively, you should also remove the windshield.

BATTERIES

Ni-Cd batteries are responsible for powering most of our R/C vehicles. These tips will help your precious packs perform as well as they should for as long as they should.

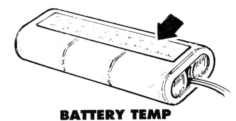

BATTERY TEMP

Here's an easy way to monitor your battery's temperature. Tape a liquid-crystal aquarium thermometer to the top of your battery pack. These thermometers are available from pet stores for about $3.

RC10 NI-CD PACK

After making a simple modification, you can fit a 6-cell, side-by-side Ni-Cd pack into your RC10. Carefully "slot" the sides as shown: drill 1/2-inch holes along the sides of the chassis, then use a Dremel cut-off disc to cut between these holes. Caution: wear safety goggles while doing this! To protect the cut edges from cracking, carefully smooth and round-off their edges, and cover them with vinyl tape. Don't make the slots any larger than necessary, and center them over the widest part of the Ni-Cd pack, as shown by the arrow.

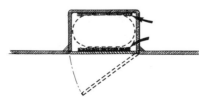

SILENCE THE RATTLES

If your hear thumps and rattles when you car goes over jumps, the culprit is probably the battery pack. Cure the problem with Velcro®—the furry side (felt or sponge rubber will also work).

BATTERY DISCHARGER

Do you have a couple of old motors lying around? If you do, wire them in parallel, lash them together and attach a suitable plug. Why? You'll be able to plug in your Ni-Cd pack to run it down for proper recharging. It's a shame to waste all that energy, though, so why not mount a couple of small fans on the shafts and use the breeze to cool the battery while it's discharging?

BATTERY CODING

A Radio Shack charger takes 6 AA cells at the same time, but it's easy to mix up your charged and discharged cells. To avoid this, use colored tape or paint to code the cells in batches of six. If you have only one color, use a series of stripes as shown here. Pack 1 has one stripe; pack 2 has two stripes, etc.

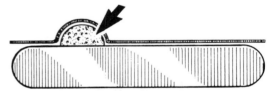

FOX 6-CELL PACK

To ensure that a 6-cell pack won't rattle around in the battery holder of your Fox, glue half a cork to the top of the Ni-Cds (arrowed) so that it fits into the recess usually occupied by the hump on a 7-cell pack.

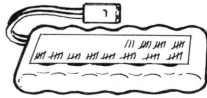

CHARGING RECORD

Stick a strip of white artists' tape along the side of each Ni-Cd pack, and write the complete history of the pack on it: the number of charge/discharge cycles, the capacity when new and the capacity following subsequent tests. This record will quickly reveal any deterioration in performance, and sub-standard packs can be kept just for practice.

CHAPTER 4

BATTERY-PACK COOLER

Did you know that cool packs take a better charge? Buy two six-pack coolers (the kind you put in the freezer). Glue them together with CA, and put them in a Styrofoam cooler, first making a hole in the foam lid for the wires. Put uncharged Ni-Cd packs in the center row and charged packs in the outer rows.

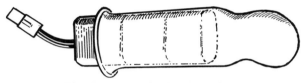

NI-CD WATERPROOFING

Waterproof your Ni-Cd pack! Take a suitable rubber balloon, stretch its neck, and slip the Ni-Cd pack inside. Close the balloon's neck tightly with a piece of cord or a twist-tie.

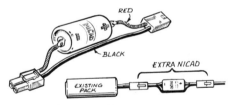

PLUG-IN SEVENTH CELL

The Tamiya is set up for 6-cell batteries, but by using a Kyosho/Tamiya male/female connector set, some no. 18 wire and an additional Ni-Cd (wired as shown), you'll be able to separate the existing connector and plug in the extra cell to obtain a total of 8.4 volts. The extra cell will ride in the hump already provided for a hump-back 6-cell pack.

HAIRDRYER USE

Disassemble an old hair dryer; discard the rectifier (found on some) and the heater, and connect a battery plug to the wires. Use this to discharge your battery pack while keeping it cool. To improve air circulation, put the pack on wooden blocks.

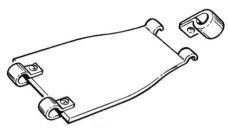

BOOMERANG BATTERY DOOR FIX

If the front tabs break off your battery door, it can be speedily fixed. First, pick up some two-wire plastic cable clips from Radio Shack. Trim off any parts of the tabs that are still on the door, and hold the door in place on the car to guide you when you drill holes for the retaining screws. Then attach the nylon clips using small machine screws (2-56 should do), nuts and washers.

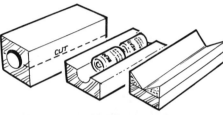

BATTERY SOLDERING JIG

Through a block of wood, drill a hole that's the same diameter as your Ni-Cd cells. Saw the block lengthways, and you'll have a useful cradle in which to hold the Ni-Cds while you assemble them into packs. Use balsa triangular stock glued to a block, too; it works just as well!

CHARGED-PACK REMINDER

If you have several packs, it's often hard to remember which one is charged—especially during the heat of battle. Write "charged" on some thick cards or plastic labels, then glue those little Velcro® circles to the backs of the labels and to the packs. As each pack is charged, slap one of your labels onto it.

BATTERY-POST ADAPTER

Small alligator clips won't fit on the posts of an auto battery, so drill a small $3/8$-inch-deep hole in the top of the lead posts, then drive in a brass screw onto which the clips will fit. To avoid corrosion, keep the screw and posts coated with petroleum jelly (don't use car grease); it won't affect conductivity.

4 BATTERIES

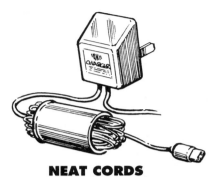

NEAT CORDS

Long charging cords tangle, and this is frustrating. Cut the bottoms off two plastic 35mm-film containers, coil the cords as shown, then push them through the containers, leaving the desired length protruding. This is neat and very effective.

FLAT BATTERY I.D.

Why didn't someone think of this before? When you remove a discharged pack from your car, just slip a rubber band over it to show that it's discharged. After charging, remove the band to show that it's ready to go.

BATTERY-PACK ARMOR

Exposed battery packs take a beating from rocks, and dents in Ni-Cd cases usually lead to internal short circuits. Put a piece of Lexan under the pack before snapping the battery retainer into place.

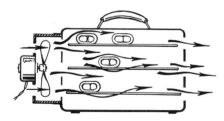

WIND TUNNEL NI-CD COOLING

Make yourself a wind tunnel, and share it with your friends. This one is a converted toolbox with suitable slots in its ends. An old fan (a stove extractor fan would be great) mounted in a box provides the airflow, while the Ni-Cds rest on cut-down barbecue grills supported on wooden blocks to promote air circulation. With a simple slide-in adapter plate, you could rapidly substitute 12V or 110V fans, depending on the power available at the track.

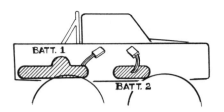

LONG-RUNNING CLOD BUSTER

Get 20-minute runs by putting a regular 7.2V flat pack in the usual position and a hump-back pack with similar voltage in the rear of your Clod. The two are joined in parallel with the Y-shaped cable adapter shown. The voltage will still be 7.2, but battery capacity will be doubled. Charge each pack separately.

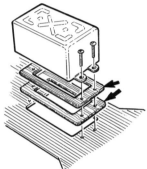

VOLTAGE BOOST FOR CLOD BUSTER

To improve the performance of your Clod Buster, fit it with an 8.4V battery. To do this, discard the plastic spacers C5 and C9 to make enough room for the battery. For a good fit, you'll need a couple of plywood shims (arrowed); you'll also need slightly longer screws to keep the battery box in place.

PACK HISTORY

Here's a way to document the history of your battery packs. Tape a label to each pack, and on it record charges, discharges and capacity/date, etc. If you cover the labels with wide, clear-plastic tape, you'll be able to use a wipe-off wax pencil.

NI-CD HOLDER FOR BENCH TESTS

This holder enables you to cycle new, unsoldered Ni-Cds before you build them into packs. The 3/4-inch PVC pipe and end caps are available from hardware stores, as are the nuts, spring, brass screws and electrical materials. Just slip the batteries into the

OPTIMA BATTERY RETAINERS

Those who are frustrated with supposedly "easy-to-use" battery straps should try this: buy some heavy-duty, 1¼-inch-diameter, rubber slip-joint rings from the plumbing department of a hardware store. Inexpensive, and much tougher than rubber bands, they'll ensure that your battery won't fall out during a tough race.

BATTERY TAGS

Save the colored plastic tags used to secure bread wrappers, etc., and use them to show the state of your battery packs, e.g., green for "charge" and red for "flat." Snap the tags over the leads as shown. The tags can be wiped clean, so you can use marker pens on them, and you can store them on a snap-on key ring.

VELCRO® CONVENIENCE

For quick trackside changes, mount your battery packs on Velcro® strips The sketch tells all.

PEAK YOUR BATTERY

To reliably ensure your battery is charged to peak, observe the voltage with a digital voltmeter. When the voltage falls by 1/10 (0.1) volt, the Ni-Cd pack can be considered peaked. In the example shown, when the voltage drops from 10.56 to 10.46, you have a peaked battery. Note how the voltmeter is wired across the battery by way of the plug. Of course, you could also wire an extra plug across the battery and plug it into that.

GRASSHOPPER NI-CD REMOVAL

Lay a piece of wide, thin tape in the battery compartment, then put the Ni-Cd pack on top of it. To remove the Ni-Cd, just pull on the tape's ends.

BATTERY-PACK PROTECTION

To protect your battery pack, use masking tape (not vinyl) to bind the cells and leads securely, then dip them into a plastic dip compound of the sort used for tool handles. One brand is Plasti-Dip, which is available at your hardware or auto-parts store. Be sure your pack has been thoroughly tested before you dip it.

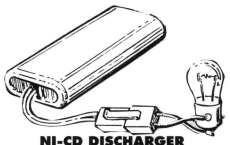

NI-CD DISCHARGER

Solder a 12V auto bulb to one half of a connector. When the bulb goes out, the Ni-Cd is "flat" and ready for its fast charge.

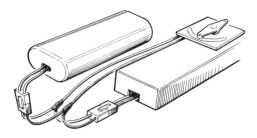

DOUBLE-CAPACITY CLOD BUSTER BATTERY

The Clod's twin motors quickly flatten a single Ni-Cd pack, but if you put two packs in parallel, you'll double battery capacity and lengthen run times. Just bare the wires, solder a second plug into the leads (as shown here), then carefully tape over the bare solder joint. Make sure both batteries are fully charged before you plug them together, or the lower one will "pull down" the other one.

CHAPTER 5

CHASSIS

The chassis is the "backbone" of every R/C vehicle, and its care is essential to keeping your vehicle in operation. These tips will help you to protect this vital component from damage, and they'll help you get it back together when it fails.

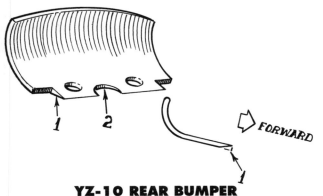

YZ-10 REAR BUMPER

Made from a JG Mfg. rear bumper, this protects the YZ-10's rear bulkhead and nearby parts from being damaged in a rear-ender. Use a file to bevel the edges marked 1 and 2. The bevels stop the bottom edge from being caught on rocks, and no. 2 also accommodates the protruding center screw.

SEAL OUT DIRT

If you seal the gap around the chassis tub with thick, self-adhesive, foam weather-stripping, it will help to keep the dirt out.

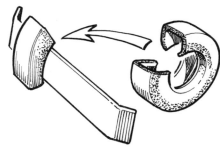

RUBBER BUMPER

Beginners can protect their cars by cutting out sections of discarded tires and securing them to the bumpers with silicone glue and insulation tape. The curved rubber pieces provide better crash protection than rigid plastic.

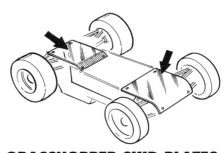

GRASSHOPPER SKID PLATES

If you drive a on a rough track, you may damage the bottom of your A-frames and gearbox cases. To protect them, cut two pieces of 1/32-inch aluminum and bend them to shape. Screw them to the underside of your car, as shown in the sketch.

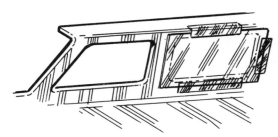

DIRT-FREE ULTIMA

The lightening holes in the side of the Ultima chassis often fill with dirt. To prevent this, tape pieces of thin plastic over the holes, or cut one long strip of plastic, and attach it with a smear of silicone sealant.

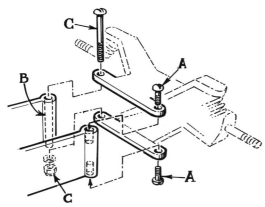

FALCON CHASSIS STRENGTHENING

Screws sometimes break out of the posts where the front-suspension assembly joins the chassis, because the four screws (marked "A") put a lot of stress on the tops and bottoms of the posts. To cure this, carefully drill through the posts from top to bottom (B), then install 1½-inch-long hardware nuts, screws and washers (C).

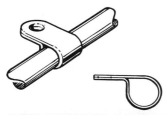

FOX BUMPER REPAIR

Does the mounting tab on the rear bumper of your Fox keep breaking off? Try this: first, clean the bumper with a file and sandpaper; then make a simple P-clip from an aluminum strip, and drill a hole to fit the mounting screw.

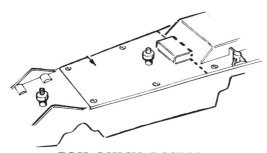

FOX QUICK ACCESS

If you need to reach the Fox servos and speed controller quickly, you'll be slowed down by 11 screws. To speed the process, cut across the radio box at the point shown. Now you'll only have to remove four screws. To keep out dirt and water, seal the joint with a strip of vinyl tape .

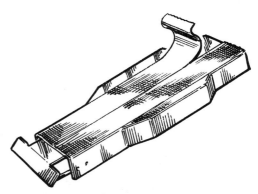

PREVENT UNDERSIDE DAMAGE

To help preserve the underside of your RC10 chassis, cover its bottom with a layer or two of duct tape.

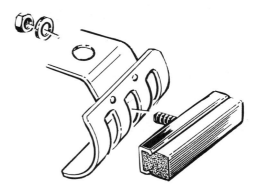

RESILIENT BUMPER

The RC10's motor guard is sensitive to rear-end collisions. To minimize the damage, bolt a standard bicycle brake pad onto the guard. The rubber pad absorbs some of the impact and protects the guard.

FIXING STRIPPED SCREWS

Have you ever stripped the threads in your plastic car chassis? If you try using a larger screw, you'll probably crack the molding, so try this: inject a few drops of CA into the hole; then wiggle a toothpick around in it to coat the area. When the glue has cured—and not before!—insert the screw.

5 CHASSIS

SECURING BATTERY BOXES

Some cars lose their batteries often, and this tears out the wires. On landing after jumps, the battery-box lid peels off. The simple solution is a patch of duct tape over the front edge of the lid and a strip over the rear edge and along the sides.

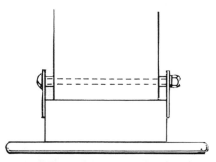

BIG BRUTE BUMPER MOUNTING

Does your Big Brute have fragile bumper-mounting tabs? Here's a solution: run a long bolt through the bulkhead and the tabs. The simplified sketch shows how.

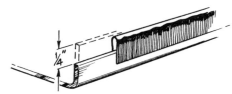

NO-SCRATCH OPTIMA CHASSIS TRAY

To prevent the sharp edges of a new chassis tray from scraping the paint on your Optima body, cut the tray approximately 1/4-inch lower, and attach electrical tape to its edges. Leave some sticking up above the chassis to act as a bumper guard.

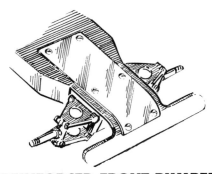

REINFORCED FRONT BUMPER

Do the front bumpers on your Tamiya Falcon break a lot? To reinforce the weak area in front of the suspension, cut a 3x6-inch piece of aluminum, and attach it to the bottom of the chassis with self-tapping sheet-metal screws. (It also doubles as a skid plate.)

NEAT HOLE-FILLING

Dirt and water can get through the unused holes in an RC10 chassis. Fill them by taping over the underside of each hole (arrowed), then squirt a blob of silicone tub sealant into each one from above. Wait until the sealant has cured, then peel off the tape to reveal a neat, flush "rivet" of silicone.

SUSPENSION & DRIVE TRAIN

Your cars and trucks encounter many obstacles and rely on their suspension to provide safe, soft landings. To "smooth out" your bumps and jolts, take a close look at the following hints.

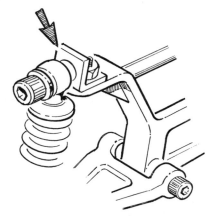

SHOCK ADAPTERS

When you switch to oil-filled shocks, you often need adapter brackets. Make these brackets (arrowed) from 1/32-inch-thick aluminum. Bolted to the existing mounts, they allow you to use regular spacers, screws, nuts and washers (which can be inserted sideways).

LUNCH BOX PIVOT WEAR

After many miles, owners often find that their car's A-frame pivots have worn considerably. Sleeves made of pieces of vinyl fish-tank hose work well to protect the A-frame bushings from wear. You could also use silicone fuel line from a hobby store.

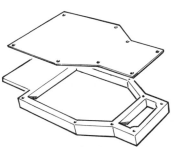

CHASSIS DIRT SHIELD

On the Frog and the Brat, the chassis bottom is open and can be damaged by stones, grit, etc. Make a simple closure using thin aluminum or plastic. Don't use screws though, because there's a danger of weakening the chassis rails. Retain the bottom with double-sided polyurethane tape

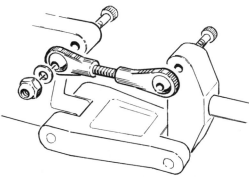

HOTSHOT CAMBER ADJUSTMENT

Usually, the camber (wheel lean-in or -out) on these cars can't be adjusted, but this simple modification changes the situation. A pair of Du-Bro ball links and a threaded rod at each wheel allow the camber to be varied. Attach the links with sheet-metal screws or (even better!) with the stout Allen-head screws, washers and self-locking nuts shown here.

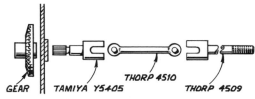

GEAR   TAMIYA Y5405   THORP 4510   THORP 4509

BLACKFOOT PLUS THORP

The tougher Thorp axles can be used on the Blackfoot if you use the Tamiya Boomerang/Hot Shot/Super Shot original gears. The gear and gear case (shown) represent all Frog-type gear cases—just order the numbered parts.

6 SUSPENSION & DRIVE TRAIN

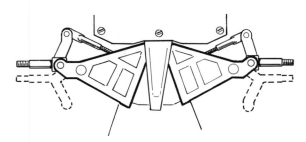

TIGHTER-TURNING PUMPKIN

Remove the A-arms from your Midnight Pumpkin, and swap them to the opposite sides so that the steering blocks and the tie rods are in front of the shocks. This will give the tires more clearance at their trailing edges and allow the wheels to have more deflection. To prevent them from rubbing on the chassis when turning sharply, make adjustments on your controller. The dotted lines show the original location of the steering arms.

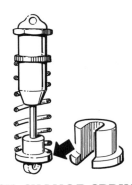

QUICK-CHANGE SPRINGS

To change springs quickly on your RC10, cut a slot in the lower spring retainer as shown. Instead of first having to unscrew the ball end to remove the spring, you can now merely lift the spring, slide the retainer out sideways, then remove the spring over the ball end. Fast and easy!

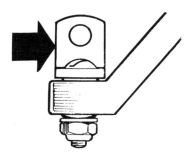

GRASSHOPPER SHOCK ADAPTER

If you want to use a wider assortment of shocks on the front of your car, bolt on these spring mounts (Grasshopper part no. G-6), using 3mm locknuts and 3x8mm screws.

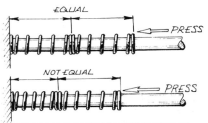

MATCH YOUR SPRINGS

If you have an assortment of spare springs of different rates, here's how to match them in pairs. Slip the springs, two at a time, over a rod or pencil, etc. Apply pressure to the end (as shown), with the opposite end against a wall or bench, measuring the spring lengths as you do so. Matched springs will be of equal lengths, while unmatched springs will be of different lengths. As you match each pair, color code them with dabs of paint just as is done with full-size race cars.

AVOID BOTTOMING-OUT

When a Grasshopper is run over rough terrain, the stock springs tend to bottom-out. The solution?—buy some Radio Shack no. 64-302 rubber grommets, disassemble the damper, slip a grommet over the retainer, and follow this with the spring. Screw the rod back onto the retainer at full tension, and the spring action becomes slightly stiffer. The grommet also serves as a rubber buffer.

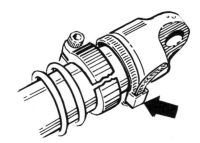

BROKEN SHOCK COLLAR

Shock collars occasionally break, and this allows the spring to slide up the shock body and alter the spring pre-load. Here's a successful temporary fix: pull a nylon cable tie tightly around the shock to keep the collar in the correct position.

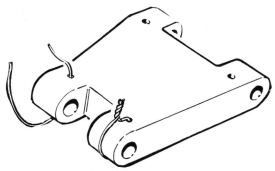

A-FRAME STRENGTHENING

A-frames on some cars have a weak spot: the pivots have been known to split. Drill very small holes where shown, then thread stainless-steel, 26-gauge safety wire through them. Twist the ends together tightly before pressing them down flat, out of harm's way. Visit your local airport mechanic—he'll probably be pleased to sell you 2 or 3 feet of the wire for a few cents, when you explain what you're doing.

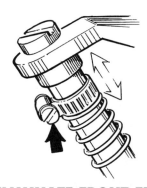

ELIMINATE FRONT-END SAG

This works well on the front ends of the Midnight Pumpkin and the Lunch Box. Pre-load the springs by adding a 5/8-inch-diameter hose clamp around the shock-absorber body, above the spring. By sliding the clamp down and then tightening it to grip the shock, you can "tune" the suspension for improved handling by varying the amount of pre-load and stiffening the springs.

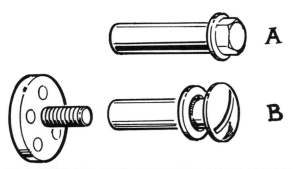

BLACKFOOT-CONVERSION AXLE BOLTS

The JG conversion kit (which allows Big Bear tires to be used on a Blackfoot) has plastic axle bolts. One-inch, aluminum, loose-leaf-binder posts (available at office-supply stores) make good replacements. Saw a screwdriver slot in the tops, and add a washer to take up the slack. (A is the original; B is the office-supply special.)

IMPROVED HORNET DAMPING

By adding a nylon front-wheel bearing above each strut spring and putting a 3mm O-ring (arrowed) above that, you can increase friction. This will substantially improve your car's damping and handling through the jumps.

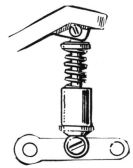

MINIMIZING SHOCK-OIL LEAKAGE

By inverting your oil-filled shock units as shown, you can minimize oil loss. They'll still leak, but not nearly as much.

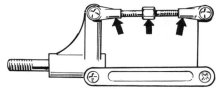

THUNDERSHOT CAMBER ADJUSTMENT

If the inboard edges of your vehicle's rear tires suffer severe wear, replace the fixed-length, plastic top links with Bolink 4-40 Adjust-A-Links and Du-Bro 4-40 Swivel Ball Links (all shown arrowed). This will allow you to tune the rear-suspension angles to your satisfaction.

6 SUSPENSION & DRIVE TRAIN

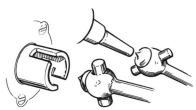

HALF-SHAFT END FLOAT

Instead of using O-rings in the drive-shaft cup to take up any end float, put a blob of silicone rubber in the bottom of the cups. You can use Permatex no. 26BR from the auto-parts store, or you can buy a tube of Loctite High-Temp RTV gasket maker (no. LHC-07). One tube treats literally hundreds of those "dogbones."

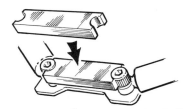

RAIDER SUSPENSION-BOLT CURE

On tough courses, the Raider's upper suspension bolts tend to bend inward. A simple cure is to wedge a 1/4-inch-thick aluminum piece between the bolt heads; you could even secure it with a wrap of insulating tape. If you can't find aluminum of this thickness, try a piece of hard maple from the model-plane section of your hobby shop.

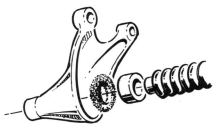

HALF-SHAFT DIRT SEAL

A common problem on the Frog is wear on the half-shafts caused by dirt under the boot in the rear arm. To solve this problem, make a small dust-seal ring out of a thick, furry, pipe cleaner; hold it in place with a short piece of rubber hose.

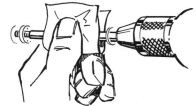

SHOCK-SHAFT POLISHING

When you're rebuilding your shock absorbers, examine the shafts for nicks and scratches, which cause leaks. Putting the shafts in a drill and polishing them with a soft cloth saturated with very fine auto polish will remove most signs of abrasion.

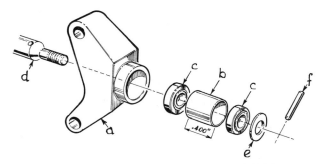

RC10 AXLES FOR THE RAIDER

The selection of wheels and tires for the Raider is limited, but with RC10 axles, you can use a variety of RC10 equipment. Bore-out the Raider hub carriers (a) to fit a 3/8-inch-diameter brass tube (b); press the tube in until it's flush, and secure it with CA. Press in the two replacement 1/4x3/8-inch RC10 bearings (c), and fit the RC10 axles (d), the thrust washer (e) and the drive pin (f). It's easy to bore-out the carriers with a hand drill if you use increasingly large drill bits (in 1/64-inch increments).

REINFORCED ANTENNA TUBE

Here's a way to keep the plastic tube that covers the antenna from being "kinked" when you flip your car. Reinforce the base of the tube by interfacing two ball-point-pen springs and forcing them over the tube and down to the base, where they're captured with a dab of tub sealant.

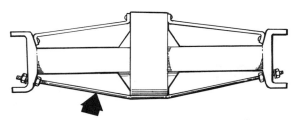

CLOD BUSTER AXLE BRACE

Hard landings often cause axle housings to break, despite the factory-installed braces across their tops. To strengthen them, cut and bend coat-hanger wire (arrowed), and position it below the axle so it firmly contacts the axle case. Thread the wire ends (4-40 wire), and screw them into holes drilled in the E-brackets, using nuts on each side. Tighten the wire with the outboard nuts, lock them tightly with the inboard nuts, and hold them with Loctite or CA.

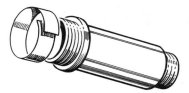

STOP SHOCK-OIL LEAKS

Do your car's shock absorbers leak oil from around their caps? Unscrew the caps, and wind a layer of plumber's Teflon tape around the thread before replacing them. This will successfully—and cleanly—stop all the leaks.

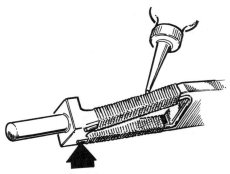

WIZARD A-ARM REINFORCEMENT

Here's a unique way to reinforce A-arms so that they won't break during a race. Bend a piece of 1/16-inch music wire (arrowed) and glue it to the bottom of the A-arm with CA. To hold the wire on the arm, wrap thin cord around it and saturate it with CA. (Remember: whenever you use a lot of CA, do it outside so that the fumes disperse quickly.)

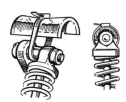

SHOCK-MOUNT PROTECTORS

The shock mounting is the highest point on most off-road buggies. As a consequence, when the car rolls over, the tops of the mounts get badly scraped. To prevent this, cut pieces of clear 3/8-inch-diameter plastic tubing and, using very small nylon cable ties (from Radio Shack), secure the pieces of tubing to the top of the mounts as shown. They're practically invisible, but provide a valuable service.

STIFFER SUSPENSION

To increase your spring rate, merely slip smaller-diameter springs inside the regular ones. Some words of advice: ideally, if the outer springs are wound clockwise, the smaller-diameter springs should have a counterclockwise wind. This prevents the coils from intertwining and becoming "solid."

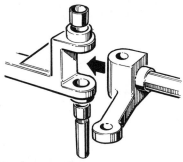

KINGPIN REPLACEMENTS

Worn kingpins? Drill out their top and bottom holes (preferably with a drill press) to 5/32-inch diameter. Press in pieces of 1/8-inch-i.d. brass tubing and add a drop of CA for good measure. Cut two new kingpins from 1/8-inch-diameter stainless-steel welding rod, reassemble the front end, check the alignment, and you're ready to race. You'll find that most of your steering slop has vanished.

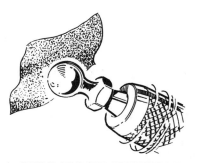

CURE TIGHT STEERING

Tight steering is frequently caused by a ball joint that's too tight. Disassemble the joint, then gently grip the threaded portion of the ball in a drill chuck. While the drill is spinning, carefully polish the ball with no. 600 emery paper until it's smooth and fit its socket.

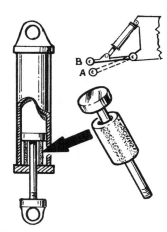

REBOUND SPRING

Putting a short length of surgical-rubber fuel tubing on the piston rod of your car's shocks serves two purposes: it acts as a rebound spring at the bottom of the unit's travel, and it alters the vehicle's ride height, which alters the roll center. The small sketch shows how: "A" shows the position of the A-frame or "wishbone" with the unmodified shock, while "B" shows the position after making the modification.

6 SUSPENSION & DRIVE TRAIN

HIGH-VISIBILITY DOGBONES
Paint your dogbones (even steering links) a bright color (e.g., yellow, white, or orange) so that if they fall off, you'll be able to see them in the dirt.

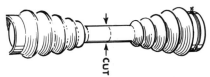

BETTER THAN BALLOONS
Instead of using balloons over your half-shafts, obtain the half-shaft boots from a Frog, cut them at the center, and slip the halves over your car's universal joints. This can be quite inexpensive, since one Frog rubber boot often yields two covers for your car—and it looks more professional!

NEAT AXLE-JOINT BOOTS
The Tamiya Frog's axle (or drive-shaft) boots are attached with unsightly nylon straps and bulky buckles. Remove the straps and cut 1/8-inch-wide bands of heat-shrink tube, which you can then shrink into the grooves formerly occupied by the straps. This looks much neater.

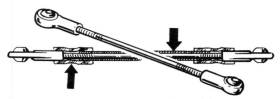

STEERING-ROD PROTECTION
To prevent rocks, etc., from damaging your steering rods (track rods), slip a piece of aluminum tube over them, leaving slight gaps at the ends to allow for adjustments. The gaps can then be covered with short pieces of clear-plastic fuel line. To improve the appearance of the rods, polish the tubes.

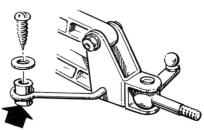

NO-SLOP SUSPENSION
Check your Frog, Suburu Brat, Monster Beetle, Blackfoot, etc. Replace the brass-tube bushing with a 3/17-inch length of silicone-rubber, model-plane, fuel tubing. This tightens the suspension, minimizes the wear at that point and improves handling.

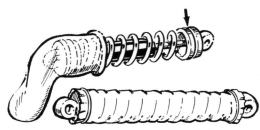

SHOCK PROTECTION
Nothing destroys shocks faster than mud and grit getting past the seals, so here's a good defense. Stretch a 1/2-inch-diameter balloon over the shock, and tie each end with cord, or use small dental rubber bands. On some shocks, it's possible to file a groove around the ends to retain the bands or thread. (See arrow.)

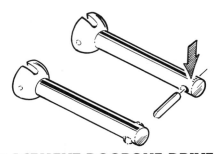

REPLACEMENT DOGBONE DRIVE PINS
To repair the drive pins of your Brute when they've been worn down to nubs, carefully file the nubs down flush, center-punch the spot, and drill holes to accept new pins. Using a Dremel grinder, cut music-wire pins, tap them into the holes, and give the shafts a couple of taps on the side, where arrowed. This pinches the pins tightly into place.

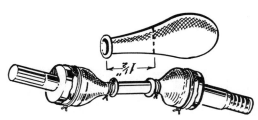

AXLE PROTECTION

Those balloons again! This time, cut them as shown, slip them over the half-shafts and universal joints of your Pegasus or Icarus after packing them with grease. Use wire cable ties to hold them in place. The axles last longer and don't attract dirt.

WORN PIVOTS

A common problem with the Hornet/Grasshopper is that the A-frame's inboard plastic pivot pins wear rapidly. To refurbish them, cut 1/4-inch-long pieces of 3/16-inch-diameter K&S brass tube, and press these pieces over the worn pivots. Then drill out the holes to suit the metal tube sleeves.

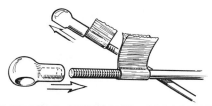

TRACKSIDE STEERING ALIGNMENT

If you have to change a ball joint, be sure not to disturb the steering alignment. Put a piece of adhesive tape around the track rod against the ball joint. When you screw on the new ball joint, stop at the tape, and it will be in exactly the same place as the one you removed. The alignment isn't disturbed, and time is saved.

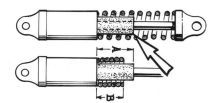

DOUBLE-DARE BUMP STOPS

Do your car's shock units bottom-out with a crash when you drive over over big jumps? To soften the impact, slip a piece of surgical rubber tubing over each piston rod. Notice that the tubing is longer (A) than the fully compressed length (B) of the spring.

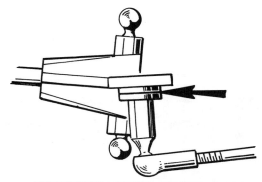

HOTSHOT BUMP-STEER CURE

The Hotshot and Supershot have a bump-steer problem, but you can significantly reduce it with this modification. Sandwich a couple of 4mm washers between the steering block and the ball connector (see arrow). Replace the stock servo-saver with a Tamiya, directly connected, servo-saver (no. 1204), and attach the links to the saver's upper left and upper right holes. You can also use Du-Bro 2mm swivel ball links (no. 368), but you'll have to *force* them onto the 3mm rod.

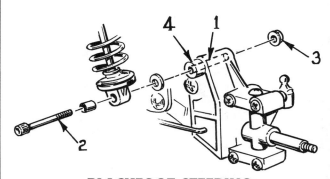

BLACKFOOT STEERING UPRIGHT IMPROVEMENT

The lower front right and left uprights tend to break because the short screw throws its entire load onto a small threaded stub. To spread the load, drill a hole (1) right through the stub and into the upright, insert a 3x12mm bolt (2), and secure this with a self-locking nut (3). Now there's less risk of damaging the stub (4). You can also use this tip on the Frog and the Monster Beetle.

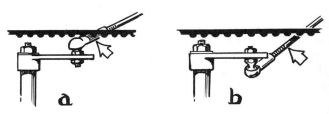

YZ-10 TIE ROD

To prevent your car's tie rod from touching the drive belt, re-route the rod, moving it from above the servo-saver arm to below it. Just move the ball link to the underside of the arm, as shown.

CHAPTER 7

TIRES & WHEELS

No matter what you do to any vehicle's chassis or suspension, the tires and wheels provide the critical link with the track. These tips offer advice on how you can improve traction and extend the life of these components.

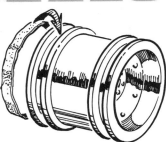

SPINNING RIMS

To prevent your car's tires from spinning on their rims, remove the tires and stretch wide, flat, rubber bands around the recesses in the rims. Then put the tires back onto the wheels. The tires will stay put.

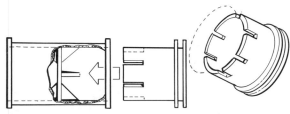

BLACKFOOT/CLOD BUSTER TIRE ADAPTATION

Now you can use the many Clod Buster tire options on your Blackfoot. Cut the outer rims off the stock Blackfoot rims, and then notch the hub to fit over the webs inside the Clod Buster hubs. Secure them with 1½-inch machine screws and nuts.

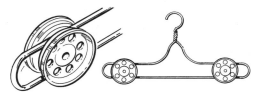

WHEEL-PAINTING JIG

To hold wheels for painting, simply squeeze together a wire coat hanger, then slip the wheels in as shown. Spray, and hang to dry.

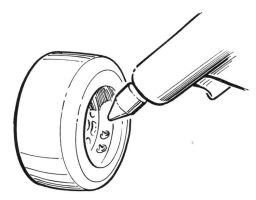

WHEEL-BALANCING WEIGHTS

Quickly attach balance weights to wheels by putting little dots of hot glue on the insides of the rims. It's certainly faster and easier than cutting off little pieces of self-stick lead.

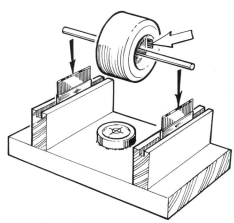

WHEEL-BALANCING JIG

If you use a table saw, it's easy to build this balancing jig accurately. Cut all the wooden parts square and cut the slots for the single-edge razor blades. Glue a bull's-eye bubble level onto the center of the jig, and place paper shims under the edge of the base until the jig is level. (Inexpensive bubble levels are available at hardware stores.) Slide the wheels onto a close-fitting spindle, lower them onto the blades, and spin gently. Determine the heavy point, i.e., the part of the tire that always stops at the bottom, and mark it with chalk. Balance the tire by sticking small bits of masking tape inside the rim as needed (arrowed).

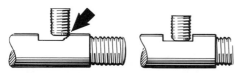

IMPROVED WHEEL SECURITY

Toyota Toms and Road Wizards occasionally shed their wheels. The setscrews don't "bottom" on the axle flat, because the slot is actually off-center, so the screws stop on the corner, as shown by the arrows. To solve this problem, carefully widen the slot using a fine file. This correction, which should apply to other cars also, allows the screws to "bottom" and tighten firmly onto the flat as in the sketch on the right.

RIM PROTECTOR

This simple device will prevent your rims from being loaded with mud. It's a plastic cap from a milk jug! Pushed into the wheel-rim well, it effectively keeps out the mud and can also be painted to resemble the rim locks and mud covers on full-scale oval racers.

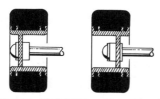

WIDER WHEEL SPACING

Turning the wheels around (inside to outside, as shown) offsets them on their axles and gives the car a much wider track. With 4WD cars, however, use caution when running off-road, because the 4WD components are now very vulnerable.

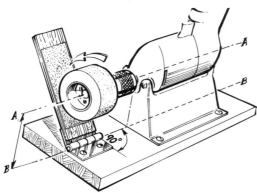

TIRE TRUING

This is a great little device for truing tires. If you don't have an inexpensive drill stand, use a vee-shaped block of wood and a large hose clip. Sandpaper boards of various grits are made up, using a progressively finer grit to finish. For really true tires, be sure axis A-A is parallel with B-B and that the hinge is at 90 degrees to B-B.

TIRE CADDY

Cut and bend a wire coat hanger so that it looks like a giant safety pin. Slip your spare tires onto a cardboard tube (this will protect the bead), close the "safety pin," and hang your tire caddy in a convenient place.

TIRE INSERT

If your monster-truck tires aren't firm enough for your needs, cut out thick, sponge-rubber donuts and stuff them into each tire. Sponge or foam plastic is easily cut with an electric knife or a band saw.

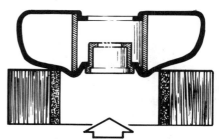

BIG BEAR TIRE FITTING

Some drivers find it almost impossible to assemble these tires and three-piece rims in such a way that all are concentric. Try this: press a roll of duct tape (arrowed) downward over the tire. This will stretch the center hole and allow the half hubs to be inserted easily.

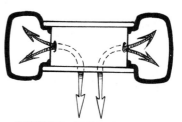

WHEEL-HUB VENTS

If your car's rear tires remain flat after the impact of a jump, drill a pair of $3/32$-inch holes in each hub to allow the air to go back in.

7 TIRES & WHEELS

CURE SIDE-WALL FLEX

If side-wall flex is a problem on your high-profile tires, here's a simple solution. Cut foam-rubber or plastic donuts the same size as the tires, then stuff the donuts inside. A band saw cuts the foam very cleanly, but if you can't manage donuts, just cut strips and wind them into a "tire" as you stuff them inside.

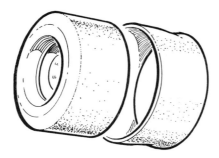

RETREADS FOR CEMENT OR BLACKTOP

True a set of old sponge tires, and then cut sections from an old cycle inner tube. Apply rubber cement to the tires, and then slide on the inner-tube sections. When the cement has dried, carefully sand off the inner-tube seam.

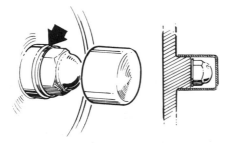

WHEEL-BEARING DUST CAPS

To prevent dirt from getting into unprotected wheel bearings (arrowed) and causing the wheels to stiffen on their axles, use some little plastic caps, and press them over the retaining nut and onto the wheel hub. A short piece of rubber tube with one end plugged with caulk would also do the job.

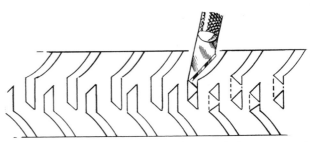

TIRE-TREAD MODIFICATIONS

Experiment with different tread configurations by using a lubricated modeling knife to slice out tread blocks. You can even try to improve on the self-cleaning ability of the tread pattern—an interesting experiment!

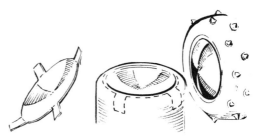

ALUMINUM HUB CAPS

Cut the domed bottoms from aluminum soda cans. Mark and trim them (as shown) so that they fit your wheel rims. Note the four tabs that are folded to fit inside the rim so the bottoms can be lightly glued with a smear of tub sealant.

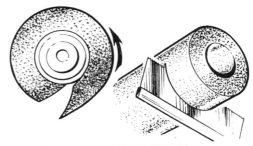

LOW-COST TIRES

Here's a source of tires for just messing about on asphalt. Obtain a length of sponge-rubber (not foam-plastic) water pipe or air-conditioner insulation, and slice it into tire-size lengths. An X-Acto or Zona saw works well. Make an angle splice as shown, wrap double-sided adhesive tape around each wheel rim, then place the tires on the rims, gluing the splice with a good silicone adhesive. Note the direction of the splice—the tires shouldn't peel off the rims under acceleration.

TRANNIES & GEARS

Getting the power from the motor to the ground is the job of the transmission, and smooth operation is essential for efficient use of battery power. These tips will shed some light on how you can get the most from your car.

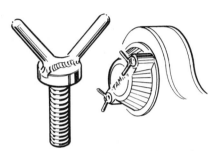

THUMBSCREWS FOR GEAR COVERS

On the Tamiya Brat, two Phillips-head screws hold the motor and pinion cover; with repeated use, their X-slots wear out. When this happens, bend a ³/₄-inch piece of music wire, and solder it into the screw slots to make handy thumbscrews that don't need a screwdriver.

SEE-THROUGH MOTOR CAP

Discard the regular opaque plastic Tamiya motor cap after first making a copy in clear plastic. The see-through cap enables you to see whether the pinion gear meshes properly with the counter gear. When it's used with modified motors, it makes gear swapping much easier.

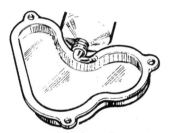

LEAKY GEARBOX CURE

Scale gearboxes leak sometimes. To minimize that problem, clean one half and apply a thin film of silicone sealant to the flange. Lightly oil or grease the mating flange, then bolt the halves together to create a thin gasket that's attached to one half only. Trim off the excess flash with a new, well-lubricated razor blade.

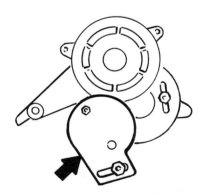

ADJUSTABLE MOTOR MOUNTS

A drawback of the Tamiya Hornet is that you can't change its pinion-gear ratios. CRP offers an adjustable motor mount for the Frog, and it works well on the Hornet without modification. Using the mount allows pinion ratios to be varied.

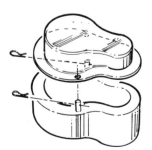

QUICK-ACCESS PINION GEAR

This gearbox cover was modified to make it easy to remove. The two 4-40 Allen-head screws were replaced with two cross-drilled headless screws. Now the pinion gear is readily accessible by pulling out two regular body clips.

CHAPTER 9

BODIES & WINGS

Correctly mounting and protecting your vehicles' bodies and wings is essential if buying new ones regularly isn't in your game plan. Listed below are a number of tips to keep your car looking sharp.

NEAT WHEEL WELLS

Cut as shown by the dotted line and then glued into your racing car, foam cups will keep dirt and dust out of the interior.

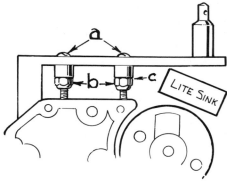

RC10 BODY-MOUNT MODIFICATIONS

If you try to install a rear body mount, you might find that it interferes with the heat sink. Screw some 3/4-inch-long screws (A) into the body mount, and hold them with self-locking nuts (B). Note the little gap (C) that allows the screws to turn freely in the mount.

WING MATERIAL

Two-liter soft-drink bottles are useful for wings. Cut out the components as shown, and you'll have a wing that's already curved. Hot-melt glue will work nicely on this plastic, and the wing can be painted or left clear (which would be unusual).

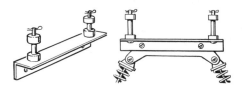

OPTIMA BODY MOUNTS

This simple system will allow Optima owners to convert a full stocker or a truck body, and it will probably work on other chassis, too. The system uses regular Parma Universal mounts with pieces of light aluminum "angle" attached to the suspension cross-members. Drill additional holes in the cross-members to allow the shocks to be repositioned and alter the car's ride height.

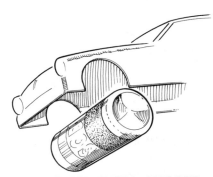

WHEEL-WELL SHAPER

You don't have to trim out wheel wells with clippers and a knife. Wrap sandpaper around a soda can; it's the right diameter, and it will give you a beautiful finish.

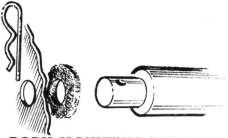

BODY-MOUNTING PADS

If your car body is painted on the inside, constant chafing during races might wear away the paint around the mounting posts. Look for a solution in the foot-treatment aisles of your drug store—felt corn pads! They come in several sizes, so you can choose one to fit over your mounting posts. If you can't find these, use self-adhesive felt and make them yourself.

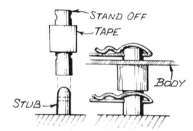

BODY LIFT FOR CLEARANCE

Here's a way to increase wheel clearance. Use short pieces of aluminum tube cross-drilled for body clips, and fit these stand-offs over the existing body-mounting stubs. Then use layers of adhesive tape to make ledges on which the body rests. It's then held by a second set of clips.

CLIP-FREE BODY MOUNTS

These were once the plastic plungers in push-up popsicles. Trim off the sides, then drill the stem to accept regular body clips. Before setting the plungers into the regular body mounts, glue Velcro® to the head of the plunger and to the inside of the car's body. Adjust to the appropriate height before inserting the retaining clips. You now have a quick-release, low-drag body mounting that's instantly accessible.

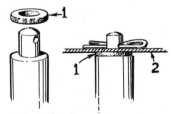

NO BODY RATTLES

Cut little rings of surgical-rubber fuel tubing, or use small O-rings. Put these on the body posts before you put the body into position, and compress them lightly before you insert the body clips.

SPEED-CONTROLLER COOLING — 1

Cut out the side windows in your car. Run a bead of hot glue or slow-setting CA around the inside, and then press in a piece of window-screen material, which will keep out rocks and most dirt. When cutting out the windows, leave enough Lexan to bend outward like a scoop, which will direct air into the car and over the controller.

SPEED-CONTROLLER COOLING — 2

Cut a little flap and bend it upward at the rear of the car, just ahead of the controller. This will scoop air over the unit.

BODY-CLIP ALTERNATIVES

You don't like those unsightly body clips? Why not get rid of them? Use washers and socket-head capscrews to attach the body to the nylon-tube stand-offs. Remove it easily with a ball-ended Allen wrench. There are also some neat chrome-plated, mushroom-head Allen screws, too. Check your electronics and hardware stores.

9 BODIES & WINGS

HOLD THOSE CLIPS!

So many drivers seem to lose their body clips, yet the solution is simple! Tie a fine nylon or Dacron thread to each clip, then tie the thread to any convenient chassis or suspension component. Alternatively, drill a very small hole in the body, then knot the thread inside the body near the clip.

BODY-CLIP ALTERNATIVE

Lost your body clips? Use a couple of bobby pins (hair grips), cut as shown.

PAINT PROTECTION

Transparent bodies are usually painted on the inside, but contact with the frame or components will soon rub holes in the paint. To avoid this, determine where the contact points are, then apply patches of vinyl tape or duct tape to prevent paint chaffing.

KEEP OUT MUD

Motoring around a wet track, this open-frame car collected a lot of mud (extra weight) in the nerf bars (arrowed). Metal from pop cans can be wrapped over the bars to fill the space. (Secure it with four small screws.)

BODY-MOUNT POSTS

Yet another simple idea! Buy Plastruct ABS tube pieces that will fit inside one another. Cut collars from the larger tube, slip them over the smaller tubes at the desired height, then apply a spot of CA. Self-tapping screws going up through the frame hold the mounts in place.

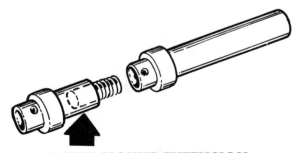

BODY-MOUNT EXTENSION

With this body-mount extension, you'll be able to use bodies of various heights on your car's chassis. First, buy a set of hollow body-mounting tubes (e.g., Parma's). Determine how much higher the extensions should be, and cut the tubes to that length. Then thread a short piece of threaded rod into the extension, along with a drop of CA. Cross-drill the top for the body clip, and the extension mount is ready to be screwed into the original mounts.

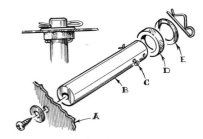

DURABLE BODY MOUNTS

This economical custom body mount has been used successfully on several dirt-oval racers. You'll need 8 feet of ¼-inch Delrin rod (B); four rubber furniture bumpers; nylon washers (E); and a regular cotter pin (C). To mount, just drill holes in the chassis plate (A) and in the end of the rod, and use a sheet-metal screw and a washer. The Delrin is virtually unbreakable in this application (unlike some other body mounts).

WING FATIGUE

To eliminate fatigue and cracking around the screw holes where polycarbonate wings are attached to the bodywork, instead of screws, nuts and washers, use pieces of double-sided foam tape. This spreads the load across the mounting points, provides cushioning against vibration and allows the tape, not the plastic, to tear away in an accident.

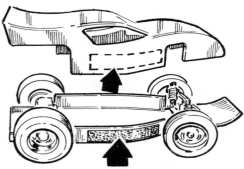

SECURE BODY MOUNTING

Instead of using the body clips, glue Velcro® along each side of the chassis and the matching part inside the body skirts. This makes a very secure, resilient mounting.

BODY-CLIP ORGANIZER

When you have to replace a body clip quickly, the spares are always lying in a tangled mess at the bottom of your tool kit. This snap-together key ring eliminates that problem, because it keeps the clips right at hand. You can also tie the clips to your car with a short piece of nylon cord—just like the full-size cars! Then, you *definitely* won't lose them!

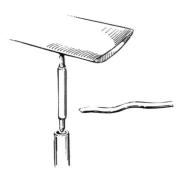

LOOSE WING MOUNT

Here's a situation where the fit of the wing-mounting wires in the mounting tubes was really sloppy. The problem was solved with a length of brass tube, which was soldered over the wires to form a sleeve and take up the excess space. As an alternative, you could curve the wires slightly to make them spring neatly into the mounting tubes.

FLEXIBLE MOUNTINGS

Crashes and roll-overs stress body-mounting points and often cause cracks to appear around them. It helps to totally isolate the body from the chassis by means of flexible mountings, and rubber grommets are readily available from Radio Shack. Open the holes in the body, then insert a grommet at each mounting point. It might also be necessary to trim the mounting posts (shown dotted). Put a washer on top of the grommet before you insert the body clips.

9 BODIES & WINGS

BODY-MOUNT REINFORCEMENT

Cut washers the size of quarters out of scraps of polycarbonate body shell, then glue them under the shell to reinforce the holes in it. Use only glue that's approved for use on polycarbonate; others might dissolve the plastic. If in doubt, use silicone sealant as a glue.

CUTTING WHEEL ARCHES

On a new body, mark the "ride center" of each wheel, then twirl a pair of dividers to scribe the wheel arch. When you've made a deep groove, flex the body to snap out the scored plastic cleanly.

BODY MOUNTS

Make your own body mounts. To a piece of brass tube, solder a washer; then cross-drill holes to accept the body clips. Next, select self-tapping sheet-metal screws that can be tapped into the tube, and mount the body posts as shown. These homemade posts are satisfactory on oval-track cars.

CRACK PREVENTION

If cracks appear near the body-mount holes, buy eyelets and fit them to the body. (Eyelet kits and punches are available from craft stores.)

CRACKED SPOILER REPAIR

This "instant fix" should prove useful at the track. Lay a piece of thin fiberglass cloth over the crack in your vehicle's spoiler—1-ounce cloth should do—and drip instant-setting CA onto it. The resulting repair is nearly invisible.

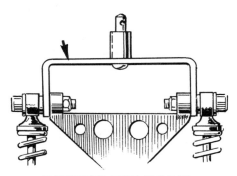

RAISING THE BODY

This is one way to custom-fit that high-clearance truck shell, and it should work on many cars. Cut a strip of hard aluminum and bend it into a broad U-shape (arrowed). Secure this under the shock-unit's bolts, and then drill it to accept one of the many available body-mounting posts. Only one post is shown here, but two would be much better.

MARKING MOUNTING HOLES

When you mount a new, painted, Lexan body, you might have difficulty seeing where you should drill the body-post holes. Shine a bright light upwards from below the body. It casts a shadow of the posts that can be seen from above, so you'll be able to mark and drill the holes.

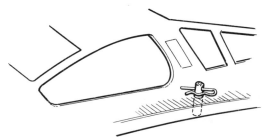

QUICK-RELEASE BODY

Some cars don't have body clips, and undoing screws is tedious and wears the screw holes to the point where they'll no longer hold the screws. Cut short pieces of 1/8-inch dowel, then twist them into the screw holes, mount the body shell, mark the dowels, then cross-drill to accept regular body clips.

DECORATIVE BODY-CLIP WASHERS

Ever looked closely at the hood clips on full-size sports cars? There's a thin, bright washer around the hole where the post comes through the hood. Now you can have the same look for your car! These washers came off the two-pronged paper studs that some people use instead of paper clips. Drilled out, they work well and look great.

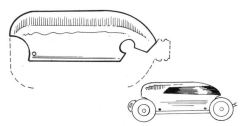

COKE-BOTTLE BODY

Now you can truthfully claim that your car is a 2-liter! This knock-around polycarbonate body is made by cutting a 2-liter soda bottle to the shape shown. To attach it to the chassis, use copper wire, plastic tube and body pins. This body lends itself to some wild paint and decal schemes!

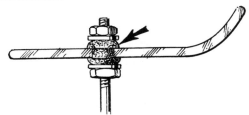

WING SAVER

Vibration and roll-overs destroy some plastic wings, but they *can* be protected. Take a couple of the spare, rubber, servo grommets that come with your radio, then put them on your wing by opening the holes to make them fit. The sketch shows the grommet (arrowed) with a washer, top and bottom. Tighten down the nut until it's *just* starting to compress the rubber, and your wing troubles will be over.

BODY-MOUNT MARKING

Before you drill holes in that brand-new, painted, polycarbonate body, you'd better be certain of the exact positions of the mounting-post holes! Put paint on the top of each post; while it's still wet, carefully put the body into place. When you remove it, you'll find four dabs of paint marking the spots where you should drill.

ULTIMA WINDSHIELD

Here's a new look for your Ultima! Use the type of transparent plastic that's used for book covers or report covers. Cut the windshield and side windows to the shape shown here. (The side tabs are wrapped around the roll bar before being fit into slots.) There's no room here to give you a full-size pattern, so use paper for your first attempts, and when you have the right shape, transfer it to the plastic. A tinted windshield would look really great!

RUBBER ANTENNA GROMMET

When a new body has been painted, its antenna hole can crack if it's left unfinished. The remedy?—buy some rubber grommets from Radio Shack, and slip one into a hole before you insert the antenna. (A smear of dishwashing soap on the grommet helps to get it into the hole.)

CHAPTER 10

PAINTING & DETAILING

Painting is one of the love/hate duties of R/C car enthusiasts. Though some enjoy it, others find it tedious and irritating. This section contains tips to make painting more enjoyable for both types of people.

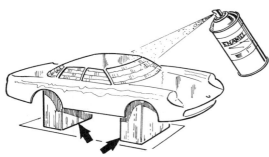

BODY-PAINTING SUPPORTS

Don't put your body shell on a workbench or newspapers to spray-paint it—it will stick to whatever it's sitting on! Raise it on wooden blocks. This trick not only prevents the body from sticking to surfaces, but it also allows you to spray it lower edges properly.

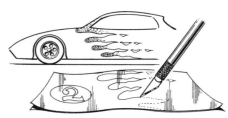

EASY MASKING

Instead of using masking tape to mask off intricate designs, obtain a length of transparent, self-adhesive, slightly tacky shelf paper. Lay out the design on paper, lay the shelf paper over this, then trace and cut using a *new* blade. Large areas can be masked quickly in one piece instead of using lots of pieces of tape.

MOLDED VISOR

Find a crystal-clear plastic bottle and, from the shoulder, cut out a realistic bubble visor. Attach it to your driver's helmet with a couple of very small screws.

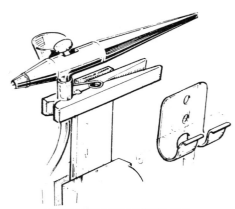

AIRBRUSH HOLDER

Airbrushes can't be set down without spills. A clothespin glued to ply and clamped in a vise will hold them nicely. Use a bent metal clip (shown) that can be operated with one hand, leaving you free to hold the painted piece!

HOMEMADE TRIM STRIPE

Lay a strip of 3M frosted parcel tape on a piece of glass, and spray it with your chosen paint. When it has dried, cut trim stripes or flashes using a sharp hobby knife. The trims are easy to position: swab the car's body with a little soapy water, then slide the stripe into place before squeegeeing the water away.

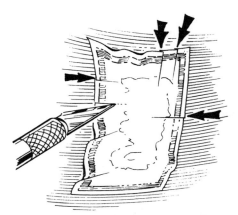

CURE FOR WRINKLED DECALS

When you apply a large decal to a curved surface, it will invariably have tucks and wrinkles along its sides. Before the decal sets, using a new hobby blade, cut slits as shown here, then firmly press down the overlaps with a moist tissue. Bubbles can be pricked with a needle and the air worked out through the hole. You could also try Micro-Sol and Micro-Set when applying decals. These products are used extensively by those who build plastic models, and they eliminate many of the difficulties encountered when applying decals.

EASY DECAL APPLICATION

This method of applying decals allows easy positioning and eliminates bubbles. Swab the area with a generous amount of a detergent/water mixture, and don't wipe it off. Immediately float the decal into place, then lay a piece of paper towel over it. Hold the towel in place while you squeegee the detergent and air out from under the decal. Always work from the center outward (as shown by the arrows), and then blot the water with a dry tissue.

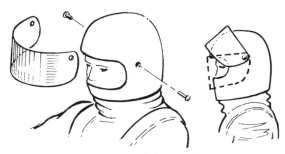

RACING VISOR

Why not give your driver some eye protection? Make this visor out of a thin, transparent-plastic sheet and a couple of straight pins cut to 1/8-inch lengths. You can tint the visor using hot Rit dye, or by attaching a piece of Zip-a-Tone transparent, colored film to it (available from art stores). Put a small drop of craft glue into each hole before you insert the pins, and then check that the visor will swivel up and down.

WINDOW MESH

Most off-road cars have no window glass, and gravel, etc., can get inside. Find some mesh from a window screen or onion/potato bags (even a piece of table-tennis netting would suit the purpose!), and glue it into place. Once in place, it looks very realistic.

SPACED STRIPES

Here's an easy way to put stripes on your car. Buy auto striping, which comes in rolls with its own backing tape. Press it into place, then peel off the backing to leave the stripes exactly where you want them. The tape is available in many color combos.

HEADLIGHT PROTECTION

Many racing cars and off-road cars have their headlights and roof lights protected with wire mesh grills. You can simulate these grills by cutting circles of window-screen material and forming them around your car's lights. Secure them with strips of clear adhesive tape.

10 PAINTING & DETAILING

EASY PAINT MIXING
To mix paint efficiently, drop three or four clean ball bearings into your paint jar, and shake the jar vigorously for 1 or 2 minutes.

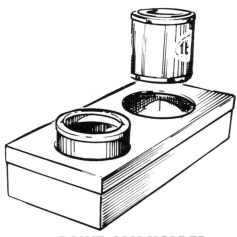

PAINT-CAN HOLDER
A cardboard box will hold small paint cans securely and prevent spills.

HOMEMADE DECALS
Cut sponsor logos out of auto magazines, then set them on a piece of double-sided adhesive carpet tape. Now, with a new blade in your hobby knife, carefully cut around the logo, peel the whole thing off the backing sheet and put it onto the side of your car. A thin coat of clear lacquer or varnish will keep the logo bright and shiny and protect it from water!

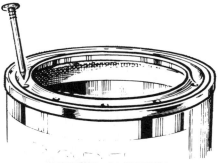

AVOID A MESS
Punch holes around the lip of a paint can to allow any overspill to drain back into the can. This also reduces splattering when you reseal the can.

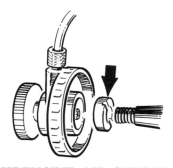

INEXPENSIVE AIR SUPPLY
Buying canned air for your airbrush can be expensive. Art stores that sell airbrushes usually sell tire adapters, too, and by borrowing the spare tire from the family car, or keeping an old inner tube for the purpose, you'll have a free air supply as close as the gas station where you inflate your tires.

POUR NEATLY
To fill small-mouthed bottles, pour liquids down a rod.

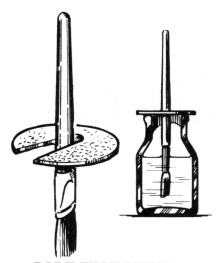

PARK THAT BRUSH

Tapered slots in metal or Formica discs will grip paintbrushes and allow them to hang clear of the bottom when parked in a jar of thinner.

HOMEMADE STICKERS

To make sponsor decals for your car, find suitable labels and wrappers, and carefully cut the logos out. Cover them with a piece of clear, adhesive plastic, and trim around them, leaving a ¼-inch margin. Apply the film-covered logos to your car's body, and carefully smooth out any air bubbles. Laminating plastic is as close as your office supply store, and one brand name is C-Line Products.

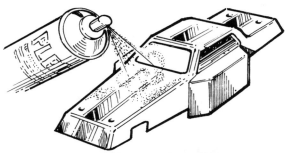

REMOVE PAINT OVER-SPRAY

Did you allow paint over-spray to get onto the outside of your race-car body? Don't resort to solvents that might damage the plastic. Instead, spray on a generous coat of Pledge liquid-wax polish, wait 1 minute, and you'll be able to remove the dust with a fingernail or Popsicle stick. Buff it to a high luster with a soft cloth. Don't use the scented Pledge, or others might think your car is a real "lemon"!

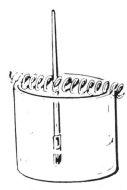

BRUSH PARKING

A spring stretched across a jar of thinner provides a convenient spot in which to park a paintbrush and keep it clear of the bottom.

COLOR YOUR DRIVER

Here's a quick way to color your driver. First spray him with matte white, then use permanent-ink markers. These permanent colors will last the lifetime of the car. Caution! If your car is glow-engine powered, spray a coat of clear polyurethane or epoxy paint over the ink, because glow fuel will smear it.

ANTI-SPILL BOTTLE HOLDER

Want to keep paint bottles and even CA bottles upright while you work? Remove the top of a large spray can, and put the bottle into the top's inner well. If the cap is made of polyethylene, you can also put some brush wash or thinner in its outer well.

CHAPTER 1

THE WORKSHOP

The appearance and performance of your racing machines reflect the state of your workshop. This group of tips from readers shows how you can keep your shop in shape and spend more time on your cars.

SPARES STORAGE

Screw as many auto-fuse tins as you need onto a strip of wood, and then label them clearly to show their contents. This setup fits neatly into a tool kit.

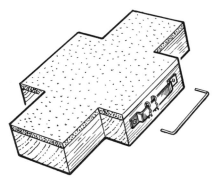

PARKING BLOCK

To prevent flat spots from forming on your tires, and to eliminate the possibility of having a runaway car if the radio is left on, cut a piece of 2x8 wood and glue $1/4$-inch foam rubber onto its top. Be sure the finished block keeps the car's wheels clear of the ground. The wire or metal strip holds body clips.

SPONGE DREMEL-TOOL CADDY

Stick all your Dremel cutters into the holes in a car-wash sponge. They'll be firmly held, yet easy to select.

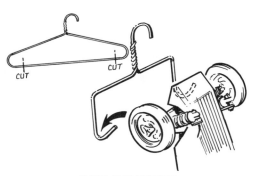

CAR HANGER

Cars occupy valuable bench space, so cut a coat hanger as shown, and make two hooks at the cut ends. These hooks should be far enough apart to engage the front or rear suspension arms. (Don't engage the drive shafts!) The hanger can hook over a nail or the wooden trim around your workshop wall.

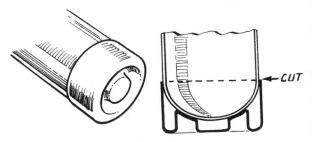

FREE PARTS CONTAINERS

Take the black plastic bases off 2- and 3-liter plastic bottles, then fill the holes. If you cut the bottle where "arrowed," you'll have a parts dish and a useful bowl in which to clean parts.

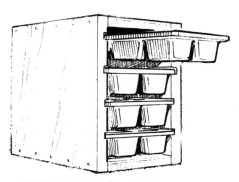

SMALL-PARTS RACK

Here's a handy small-parts rack made of a wooden box and plastic ice-cube trays. The sides of the box can be grooved to take the trays; or you could make the box larger and glue in wooden runners.

PARTS CADDY

To make sure parts are conveniently to hand and in sequence, keep them in egg cartons. When working with a kit, tape the labels from the bags into the lid in logical order, and everything will be handy and well-organized.

"THIRD HAND"

These very useful "third hands" are made of coat-hanger wire and bulldog clips soldered together. You could make several, file the jaws off some, and glue in balsa pads (useful when soldering small pieces of wire assemblies and in tricky gluing jobs).

PARTS ORGANIZER

It's always difficult to keep track of loose parts when assembling a kit. To make it easier, transfer all the bagged parts into clear-plastic 35mm film containers, and then tape the label from the bag onto the appropriate container.

STORAGE BOXES

Very handy storage boxes can be found at most photo processing stores in the form of 2x2-inch slide containers, and you might get them for nothing! Why not put together a rack using foam board or corrugated card?

TOOL CADDY

A household scrub brush makes an excellent small tool caddy for the workbench. For greater convenience, it can be secured with a wood screw or double-sided servo tape.

11 THE WORKSHOP

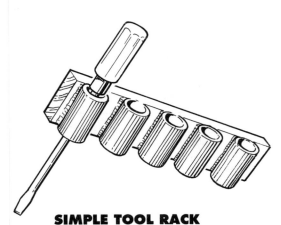

SIMPLE TOOL RACK

This very simple tool rack is made of old garden-hose sections that have been "hot-glued" to a piece of wood. Make it to any length, and nail it to the wall, or to a handy beam.

WORK PAD

A square of foam-rubber carpet underlay placed beneath your car during assembly or repair will prevent scratches and will catch and hold any dropped screws, clips, washers, etc.

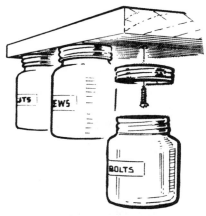

SMALL-PARTS STORAGE

Screw the lids of empty jars to the underside of a shelf, and hold small parts in the jars. Recycling!

SOLDERING HOLDER

While you're soldering, hold small parts securely by embedding them in sand.

WORK LIGHT

A pen light and suitable shim taped to a Dremel grinder will help you to direct light into dark corners.

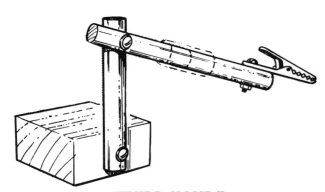

"THIRD HAND"

Here's another "third hand." You'll need a wooden block, a dowel, screws, nuts and an alligator clip. An additional cut and a tight plastic sleeve (dotted) would allow rotation, too!

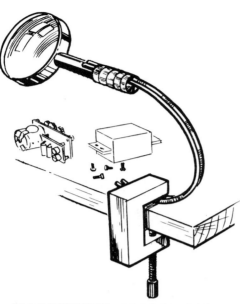

MAGNIFYING-GLASS HOLDER
Heavy electrical wire or coat-hanger wire taped to a magnifying glass helps with fine work.

SOLDERING-IRON REST
This soldering-iron rest can be made in a jiffy out of a coat hanger.

SOLDERING-IRON REST
Here's another neat soldering-iron rest made with coat-hanger wire, but this one rests on a tin lid.

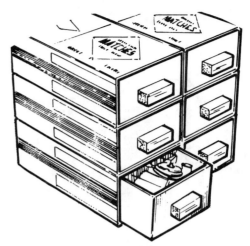

SMALL-PARTS BOXES
These small-parts drawers are large matchboxes glued together. Contact paper covering will improve the unit's looks.

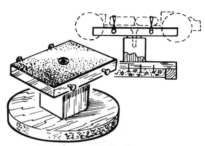

SIMPLE TURNTABLE
It's much easier to work on your car if it's supported. Attach your car to this simple turntable with rubber bands. The base can be built up to provide a recess into which short nails can be driven. The nails key into ordinary mortar (cement) that adds weight to the base. Note the rubber pad on top of the turntable.

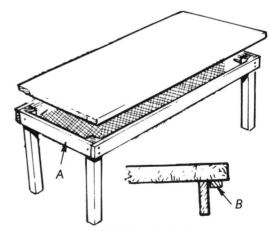

WORK TABLE
Reject hollow doors are relatively inexpensive and make excellent work tables. This one is made with 1x4-inch framing and 2x2-inch legs. Only the pieces marked "A" are screwed to the legs; the side rails may be unscrewed for storage. The door just rests on the frame and is held in position by strips (B) that have been nailed and glued to the underside in four places. Be sure all is flat!

11 THE WORKSHOP

TOOL CADDY
A tool caddy with painted silhouettes reminds you that you're about to leave a tool behind at the track. The board can stand as shown, or be a pull-out shelf in your toolbox.

ROTATING WORK STAND
Use double-sided tape to mount your work stand on a Rubber Maid "Lazy Susan," and you'll have a useful, lipped tray that holds parts.

DYE STRAINER & STORAGE
Cut a 2-liter soda bottle as shown, then drill small holes in the cap. Put the cap back onto the bottle, which fits perfectly into the top of an empty milk jug. After dyeing plastic parts, carefully pour the dye into the bottle funnel, and you'll be able to pick out the parts easily. The dye can be stored in the jug for future use. No muss; no fuss!

MAGAZINE FILES
Here's an inexpensive way to preserve your valuable copies of *R/C Car Action* magazine. Cut laundry detergent boxes as shown, and cover them with shelf paper or wallpaper. Write the magazine title and year on the front panel.

KNIFE HOLDER
The simplest way yet to stop that hobby knife from rolling off the workbench!—two modeling pins.

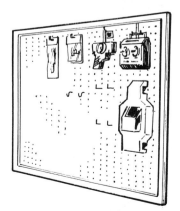

PEG-BOARD STORAGE
Mount a peg board above your workbench, and hang cars, accessories and other paraphernalia on it.

THE TOOLBOX

When you're dealing with parts as small as those found on our R/C vehicles, the right tool isn't always available. Read this section to discover how you can get around some of those "special tool" situations.

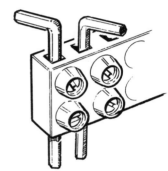

ALLEN-KEY STORAGE

Keep your Allen keys handy and secure by gluing a Radio Shack terminal strip to the side of your toolbox (hot-melt glue works well). Now you can drop the keys into the wire slots, and when it's time to go home, twist a terminal screw to secure each key.

ALLEN-WRENCH MODIFICATION

Buy some inexpensive file handles, then cut your Allen wrenches as shown, leaving just a short 90-degree bend. Epoxy the bent end securely into the handle, and carefully check the alignment. You'll have wrenches that are easier to use and less likely to be lost.

BALL-LINK REMOVER

Saw and file a slot of a suitable size in the blade of an old, large screwdriver, clean off the burrs, and you'll have an effective tool for popping off ball links without splitting the sockets (as usually happens when you try to twist them off).

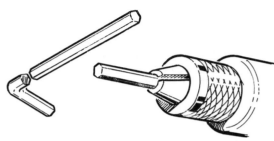

POWER-DRIVEN ALLEN KEYS

Speed up your pit work by cutting the 90-degree bend off your Allen keys. Once done, you'll be able to insert the keys into the chuck of a cordless electric screwdriver. This can also be done with Phillips-head screwdrivers.

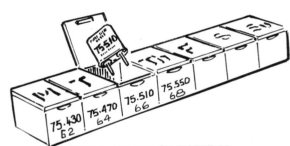

CRYSTAL PROTECTION

Radio crystals are delicate, and they crack if badly handled. For maximum protection, store each pair in a seven-day pill container, with a little foam or tissue between them. Find these useful plastic containers at your drugstore.

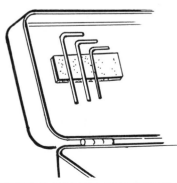

MAGNETIC ALLEN-WRENCH HOLDER

Stick a piece of Radio Shack's self-adhesive magnetic strip inside the lid of your toolbox to hold Allen keys, knife blades, washers, nuts and more.

12 THE TOOLBOX

SCREW STARTER

A short piece of surgical-rubber fuel tube over the tip of a screw-driver holds screws securely while you put them into hard-to-reach places.

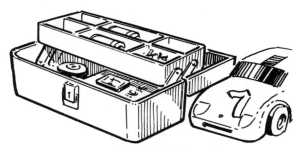

TRACK BOX

Need an inexpensive "track box"? Your local dime store has plastic fishing-tackle boxes in which you can store and sort all kinds of useful stuff, and there's room for a charger and sandwiches in the bottom!

RC10 AXLE-NUT WRENCH

To simplify the job of removing RC10 front-axle nuts, heat a regular 7/32 ignition wrench, and bend it as shown.

ALLEN-KEY MARKINGS

Dropped Allen wrenches can be difficult to spot if they fall to the ground. Wrap brightly colored adhesive tape around their shafts, or paint them.

EMERGENCY SCREWDRIVER

Only recommended for emergencies! If you lose a screwdriver at the track, a modeling knife with the blade reversed in the chuck may be enough to turn light screws.

ALLEN-KEY REPAIR

Restore worn hexagonal Allen keys. Use a Dremel cut-off disc to remove the worn parts and leave crisp, sharp edges.

TOOLBOX ORGANIZATION
To organize your toolbox, put strips of self-adhesive magnet in the bottom of each compartment, and the screws, etc., will stay put.

DRILLING HOLES
Drilling neat, round holes in plastic body shells is hard to do if you don't know how to grind the correct drill point. Why not drill a small pilot hole first, then use a tapered reamer to open the smaller hole? The result will be a neat hole (no ragged edges or egg shapes!).

EASY SHOCK BALANCING
Use one screwdriver to push down on the spring clamp and another to tighten the screw. Notice how the first screwdriver has calibration marks scratched or filed into its shaft; this makes it easy to gauge the amount of spring pre-load on each shock.

HANDY CLAMP
A rubber band around its handles turns pliers into a clamp.

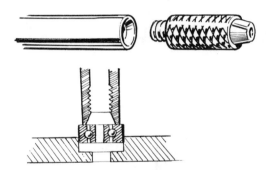

BEARING PRESS
If you want to press in new bearings, try this. Take the collet off a no. 2 X-Acto knife; the handle is exactly the right size to fit nicely on the outer track of the bearings, and the bearings won't be stressed by your pressing on the inner track. You'll be able to press in new bearings squarely, without damaging the fragile balls.

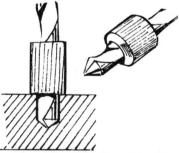

DRILLING BLIND HOLES
If you need to drill a hole that doesn't go all the way through, measure along the drill bit to the depth of the required hole, wind a strip of masking tape around the bit at that point, and then drill into the material until the tape just touches its surface.

12 THE TOOLBOX

BODY-CLIP PULLER

If your big hands have trouble pulling small body clips, try this little puller made out of a nail. After removing the head, glue the nail into a dowel handle. Use a Dremel cut-off disc or a small saw to notch as shown. A crochet hook would also make a good puller. You could also magnetize the nail so that you don't lose the clip. (Why not *tie* the clips to the car with fine nylon monofilament?)

SMALL-PARTS HOLDER

A magnetic door-closer strip fastened to the inside of your toolbox will hold a handy assortment of pins, screws, washers, etc.

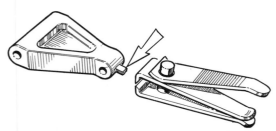

TRIMMING MOLDED PARTS

Instead of slicing and filing, try using nail clippers to remove flash or molding gates. They trim flush and "clean as a whistle."

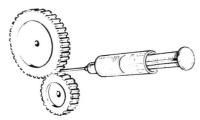

SAVING MONEY ON GREASE

Are you tired of paying high prices for molybdenum grease? Auto-parts stores sell large containers of it for about $4. Buy a syringe from a drug store, and use it to dispense the grease accurately.

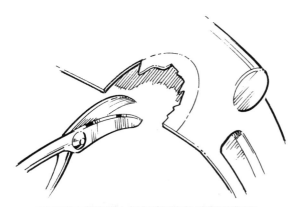

TRIMMING AROUND CURVES

It's almost impossible to do a good job of trimming out the fender wells on polycarbonate car bodies, but there's an ideal tool for the job: a pair of curved nail scissors help you cut into hard-to-reach places. (No need to buy the most expensive!)

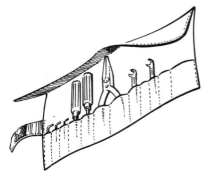

DENIM TOOL ROLL

An old pair of jeans, some wide fabric tape, a piece of Velcro® and a little time on the sewing machine, and you'll have a handy quick-pick tool roll that's very useful on the pit counter.

SCREW HOLDER

The old trick of using rubber fuel line to hold screws on a screwdriver while reaching into awkward places also works extremely well with Allen wrenches.

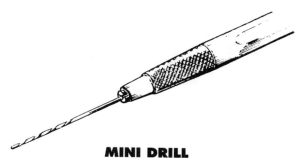

MINI DRILL

Tiny drills can be held in the chuck of a mechanical pencil, then twirled to drill holes. This is an accurate, reliable way to drill small models and plastic kits.

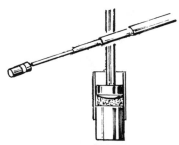

MAGNETIC RETRIEVER

Epoxy a small Radio Shack button magnet to the end of an old antenna, and it becomes a useful tool for retrieving dropped screws, etc. Masking tape applied around the magnet forms a dam to retain the resin while it cures. Note the gap between the magnet and the antenna to prevent the latter from becoming one long magnet.

PARTS CAROUSEL

Small jars, with their lids secured under the four wooden arms of this invention, rotate on a piece of broom handle to bring supplies conveniently to hand. Why not put another one on top, using a length of threaded rod down through the center? Two tiers will occupy the space of one.

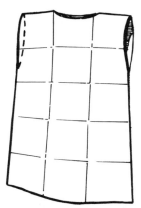

QUICK RAIN JACKET

Carry a garbage bag; slit as shown, it makes a fine rain jacket for those summer showers.

EXTENDED DRILLS

Extend a drill bit to reach inaccessible places by silver-soldering it into brass tube of the appropriate size.

CHAPTER 13

GLOW ENGINES

Do little problems stop you running your gas-powered car? Try following the advice in this section; you'll find that gas engines are easier to run than you thought.

INTAKE TIPS

A cap from a toothpaste tube serves many functions, e.g., with its center removed and a fine piece of mesh glued in to make a filter, it becomes a dust cover for the engine intake when the engine isn't running, or an intake extension for a cowled engine. (It should fit snugly.)

STARTER BENCH

Make a simple wooden bench, bolt your starter to it with U-bolts, attach a utility box that contains a household light switch, and mount your battery on the space remaining. To avoid accidents, secure the battery to the bench with a suitable clamp or rubber strap. Raise the bench on a simple folding sawhorse arrangement to a height that's comfortable.

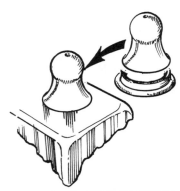

EFFICIENT SELF-PRIMER

Install a cut-down baby-bottle nipple on a gas cap. Make sure the hole in the nipple is large enough to ensure an adequate gas flow to the engine.

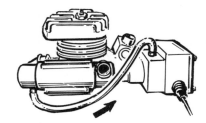

GEARBOX IMPROVEMENTS

This sketch shows how it's possible to screw a pressure fitting into the muffler and the power input side of the transmission. To continually lubricate the gears, the silcone rubber tube sends exhaust-oil mist to the gearbox. An additional benefit is that the gearbox is lightly pressurized, and this helps to keep out dirt and water.

ASSAULT FUEL FILTER

The neatest place for a fuel filter on the Assault is between the wing supports (when you've cut the fuel line). In this position, the filter is easily accessible for cleaning, but it's also protected. (The arrow shows the filter.) This should work on many other gas-powered cars.

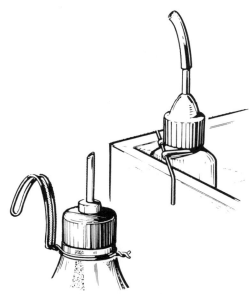

PRIMER BOTTLE HANGER

Keep primer bottles out of the dirt. To hang the primer bottle on your toolbox, twist a piece of wire or use a rubber band to attach the wire.

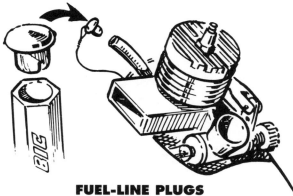

FUEL-LINE PLUGS

Ball-point-pen plugs make ready-made fuel plugs that are ideal for pressure lines. Drill a hole in the plugs that have wider flanges, and insert a retaining wire so that it's easy to find if you drop it.

CLUTCH-SPRING IMPROVEMENT

To combat clutch-spring breakage, solder little music-wire loops onto each clutch shoe. Cut two nails 1/4-inch long and drive them into the back plate to serve as pivot pins and shoe retainers.

FUEL FILTER

You'll find dirt and sludge at the bottom of large fuel cans, so to avoid contaminating you fuel tank or filters, strain your fuel through a coffee filter that's set in a funnel. (A staple or two keeps the filter paper folded.)

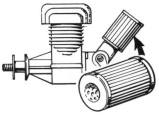

CARBURETOR AIR FILTER

Go to your auto-parts store, and search through the rack of gas-line filters. Find one that will fit on your carburetor (a Purolator P-119 does the job nicely).

13 GLOW ENGINES

STARTING NI-CD
Make your own "hang-on" Ni-Cd battery. Solder an insulated, heavy copper wire loop to the negative end of a 4000mAh, D-size, Ni-Cd battery, then tape as shown.

NEAT STARTING BATTERY
Tape the glow clip securely to the Ni-Cd, and you'll have no trouble with broken connections.

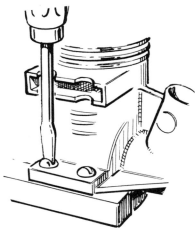

SCREW ACCESS
For easy access to the mounting screws on some engines, notch the exhaust stack.

AIR FILTER
Use three layers of nylon hose to make a carb air filter. There's no measurable power loss.

SPRING REPLACEMENT
A short piece of surgical-rubber fuel tube is an excellent substitute for that lost needle-valve spring.

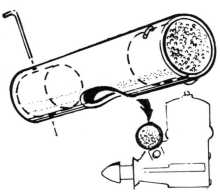

CARB AIR CLEANER
To make an efficient air cleaner, plug the ends of a piece of rubber tubing with slugs of porous sponge-rubber foam. Make a hole in the center, and snap on the air cleaner over the carburetor.

FUEL-LINE PROTECTION

To avoid melting your fuel lines, slip a couple of appropriately sized washers over the lines to act as spacers and keep them away from heat. A ball-point-pen spring will also work.

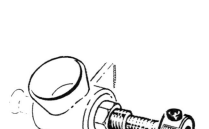

NEEDLE-VALVE REPAIR

Here's a repair for a broken needle valve: tighten a wheel collet onto the needle stem.

CAR STARTER

A bicycle turned upside-down can be used as a race-car starter.

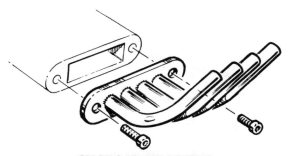

CUSTOM HEADERS

Custom headers are easy to make by bending soft copper tubing and silver-soldering them into a $3/32$-inch brass plate. To temper it, heat to cherry red and immediately drop into cold water.

FUEL-LINE SAFETY

An additional $1/4$-inch collar of fuel tubing stretched over the fuel line makes for a tight fit on tank tubes.

CAN CAP HANDLE

Solder a 3-inch nail to a spare fuel-can top. Transfer the top to a new can and screw it down tightly. The T-bar makes it easy to unscrew now! Fuel tubing protects your fingers.

13 GLOW ENGINES

FLEXIBLE NEEDLE VALVE

A flexible needle prevents accidental breakage. Cut through the needle stem, then solder a ball-point-pen spring between the halves. You can also make superb flexible extensions this way, using coiled, expanding curtain wire.

CHEAP FUEL PUMP

Make a fuel pump with a short piece of aluminum tube, a section of gas-proof fuel line, a gas-proof bung, a fuel filter, and an inexpensive siphoning pump.

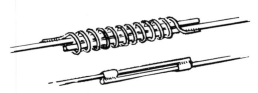

THROTTLE OVERRIDE

Install a spring override to the throttle to allow "blipping" without turning on the radio. It also prevents servo-motor stalling if it overruns throttle travel. To keep rods in line, additional bushings may be required as shown.

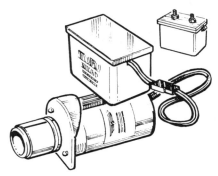

NI-CD PACK

Replace your starter-box battery with a much lighter Ni-Cd starter pack from an electric-start mower, and buy a matching plug for the starter cable from an auto-parts store. Alternatively, put two bolts through a piece of plywood to form binding posts to which the starter can be clipped, then glue the plywood to the top of the pack with tub sealant. To prevent sparking, cover the plugs with plastic or dowel caps after use.

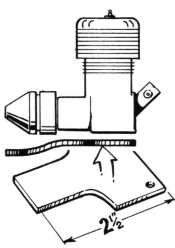

SKID PLATE

Do you have a Kyosho Assault? Has the suspension ever bottomed-out in a hole so that the starter cone hit the ground and sometimes stopped the engine? Try this cure: cut thick plastic to the shape shown, form it over heat, and screw it below the engine.

MAINTENANCE

Maintenance is one of the most important parts of running an R/C vehicle. Spend enough time on this, and you'll be more successful at the track. These tips can help simplify the job.

REAR WHEEL REMOVAL

Removing the rear wheels of dune buggies (e.g., the Tamiya Rough Rider) can be a little tough on the thumbs. Put a coin—a quarter works well—on top of the axle. Apply your thumbs to the coin, and the wheel pops off—no pain!

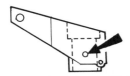

RC10 BEARING CLEANING

To make cleaning easier, drill a $3/32$-inch hole through the side of the rear hub carrier (arrowed). Insert the nozzle of a pressure can into the hole, and blast dirt out of the bearing in the opposite direction from which it entered. Then spray your favorite lube into the hole, and seal it with tape or a "plug" cut from a toothpick.

HIGH-PRESSURE BEARING CLEANER

Push a piece of surgical-rubber tube over the end of a turkey baster, fill the baster with mineral spirits, and force a bearing into the tube. Squeeze the bulb and blast out the dirt!

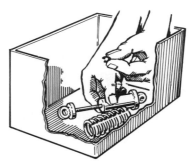

CAPTIVE C-RINGS

To prevent C-rings from catapulting away and being lost while you try to install them on the shock units, work with your hands and the shock units inside a large cardboard box. If the C-rings jump off, they'll just bounce off the inside of the box and stay there.

PARTS-CLEANER BASKET

Save that old coffee scoop, and drill lots of holes in it. Put small parts inside the scoop to wash them, and they won't get flushed down the drain. Polyethylene scoops are better than polystyrene ones, because chemical solvents don't dissolve polyethylene.

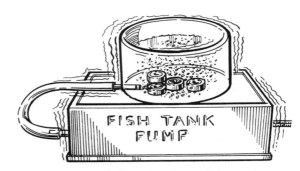

BUBBLING BEARING CLEANER

Here's an ingenious bearing cleaner. Immerse your dirty bearings in a suitable container of solvent, and attach it to a fish-tank pump. The air bubbles will agitate the cleaning solution, and the bearings will literally have the dirt shaken out of them!

14 MAINTENANCE

LATCH REPAIR

Try this if the battery-cover latch of your Hornet pops open at the slightest provocation because the latch is worn and bent back through constant use. Remove the hatch and hold the inside face of the latch over a small flame, gently bending it forward as the plastic softens. When the plastic has cooled, it will be back in alignment with the rest of the cover and as good as new.

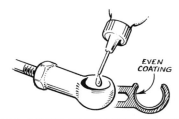

BALL-LINK REJUVENATION

If your car's ball links have slackened, temporarily tighten them by popping the ball link apart and dropping a spot of CA into the socket. Rotate the socket so that the inside is evenly coated with CA, then tap the link so that the excess runs out. (Wear eye protection for this job.) When the CA has cured, snap the ball back into the socket. Repeat the process until the ball joint is tight.

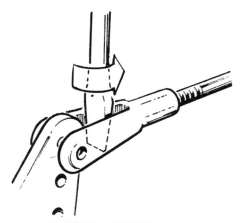

CLEVIS OPENER

Metal or nylon clevises pop open easily with a twist of a small screwdriver.

REFURBISH PLIERS

Worn teeth on pliers can be refurbished to some extent by using the Dremel Cut-Off wheel in the Moto Tool.

HIGH-PRESSURE AIR SOURCE

A high-pressure air source is very useful at your pit counter. It's great for blowing dirt out of your car. You can buy inexpensive, empty, Freon containers from your local air-conditioning man and conversion kits of a gauge, hose, relief valve, etc., from auto-parts stores. When converted, you can charge the portable air bottle at a local service station if you don't own a compressor.

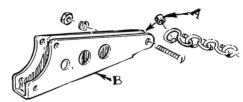

SLED-PULLING CHAIN MOUNT

This chain mount was made with a Midnight Pumpkin wheelie bar and a suspension-unit spacer (A). The spacer goes through a chain link, then both are put between the side plates of the wheelie bar (B), where they're secured with a machine screw, a lock-washer and a nut. The bar can be mounted in the usual position on the drive case.

ORGANIZED WRENCHES

To speed up maintenance and pit work, change all the screws on your car to the Allen-head variety. Using a Q-Tip, color-code them—one color for each size. Then color-code each size of Allen wrench to match, and eliminate all the fumbling for the correct-size wrench.

ELECTRICAL

Do you have a problem with your speed controller or your battery pack?—or is something else the cause of your difficulties? Here are some tips to help you avoid electrical problems and repair electrical systems.

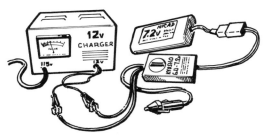

12V CHARGING

For bench charging where a 12V source is required, use a regular 12V automobile charger. Just be careful to observe the usual red-to-red and black-to-black polarity of the leads, and be sure the clips are insulated (not shown here), or you'll ruin your equipment.

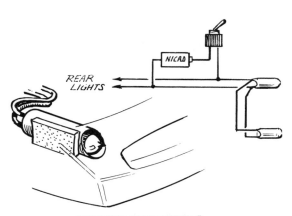

NIGHT DRIVING!

Want to run at night? Buy Radio Shack's 6V, 60mAh Mini Lamps in red, yellow and green. Drill the car's body, glue in a drinking straw or another suitable plastic tube, and insert the lamps. Hold each lamp with a small dab of silicone glue, but keep glue that smells like vinegar off copper wires, because it will eat them! Double-sided foam tape will also hold the tubes in place against the side of the body. Wire them to your Ni-Cd battery through a small switch, or use a separate Ni-Cd for them.

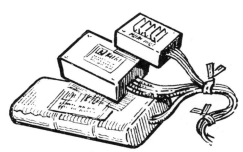

ORGANIZED WIRES

Apart from looking messy, having a twisted mass of wires under the bodywork will lead to "fatigue breaks" in the wire—the result of constant movement. Use twist-ties to hold those wires neatly.

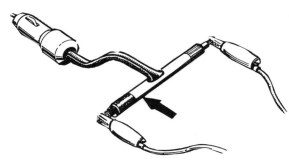

CIGARETTE-LIGHTER ADAPTER

Now you can connect your 12V charger to a cigarette lighter without changing the useful alligator clips. Cut a Radio Shack auto-lighter replacement power cord (no. 270-021), and feed the wires into a plastic tube (e.g., a large drinking straw) so that the positive and negative leads come out of opposite ends. The tube keeps the alligator clips apart and prevents a hazardous short circuit. Color the ends of the tube red and black to match the appropriate wires.

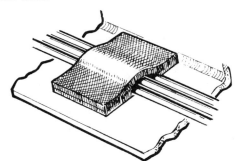

NEAT WIRING

Stick a piece of Velcro® to a suitable place on the chassis, then neatly arrange your wiring on it, and trap the wires with the mating Velcro piece. Wire connections that are held firmly are less likely to fracture.

15 ELECTRICAL

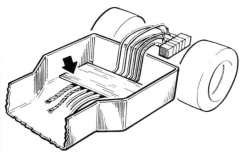

TIDY WIRING
On most cars with a bathtub chassis, the battery pack is installed under a bird's nest of wires that has to be negotiated when you remove the pack. Solve the problem by jamming a piece of thin wood (e.g., 1/8-inch-thick balsa) down firmly between the chassis sides with the wires laid neatly underneath, as shown in the drawing. You'll be able to remove the battery pack without having to fight your way through all those wires.

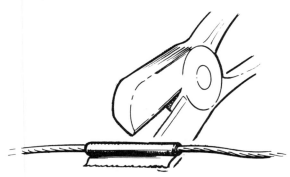

NEAT WIRE CULLING
To prevents strands from unwinding, wrap lead-out wire with tape before you cut it.

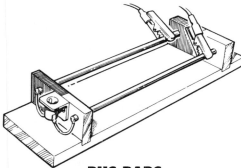

BUS BARS
At races, friends often share a 12V auto battery. This bus-bar system makes it easier to attach a charger. Two pieces of copper rod or pipe are held in a wooden stand that's colored red on one half and black on the other to show the positive and negative bars. Heavy wire and spring clips connect the bars to the auto battery, and the chargers being used are then clipped to the bus-bars. Notice the cigarette-lighter socket that's wired across the ends of the bars to cater to any charger with a suitable plug. Make sure the copper rods are far enough apart to prevent shorting from one clip to the other.

CONNECTOR PIN REMOVAL
Buy pieces of brass or aluminum tube—5/32-inch i.d. for female pins and 1 1/8-inch i.d. for male pins. As shown here, pressing the tube over the pins will compress the barbs and allow the pins to be extracted through the wire entry-side of the plug body.

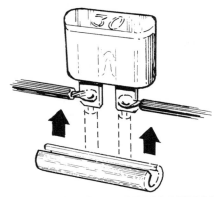

NEATER FUSE INSTALLATION
On some speed controllers, you must solder a fuse into the lead, as shown by the dotted lines in the illustration. If your wiring doesn't lie neatly in your car, re-solder the leads in the way shown here. To guard against short circuits, split a piece of gas-model fuel line and put it over the connections.

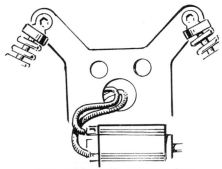

RC10 WIRE ROUTING
To prevent wires from being chafed on the rear tire, run them inside through the large hole in the rear shock-mount bracket.

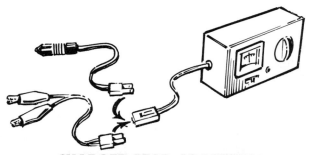

CHARGER-LEAD ADAPTERS

If you want to plug your charger into your auto's cigarette lighter and also clip it to the car's battery sometimes, try this. Cut the charger power lead, and insert a plug that will accept adapters: one for the lighter socket and one with crocodile clips that can be attached to the battery posts.

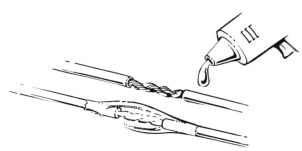

INSULATING SOLDERED JOINTS

After soldering two wires together, instead of using the customary insulating sleeve, run glue from a hot-glue gun over the connection, and overlap the insulation to support and strengthen the connection.

BROKEN HORNET WIRING

The constant up-and-down movement of the motor and gearbox causes motor-wire fatigue fractures. Lengthen the wires so that they can be wrapped in a spring-like coil before they're soldered to the motor tabs. This will allow them to flex freely—especially if you use highly flexible wire. Strengthen the soldered connections by slipping a heat-shrink sleeve over the wire and the tab.

EASY PLUG ACCESS

If you cut away the screen on one side of your car, the battery leads will be able to hang out through the window until you're ready to race; then you can plug them together and stuff them back inside.

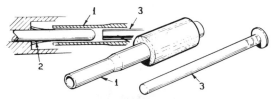

PIN REMOVAL

With this little gadget, you'll be able to compress the barbs of a pin (2) and then push the pin backward out of the plug body. The barb compressor (1) is made of $5/32$-inch brass tube and, for convenience, it's glued to a dowel handle. The end of the tube must have a slightly smaller outside diameter, so file it, or rub it with a strip of emery paper. The pin pusher (3) is a convenient box nail with its point ground flat.

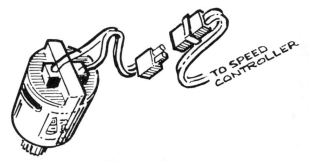

QUICK-CHANGE CONNECTORS

When servicing your cars at the track, being able to quick-change your motors is a big plus. Install Tamiya connectors in the motor leads. If you put the male plug on the leads, you'll be able to plug your motor directly into the battery for no-load testing.

CHAPTER 16

CLEAN UP

Cleanliness is next to you know what, and there are ways of making clean-up more tolerable. Here are tips on how to make your car sparkle.

CLEANING-FLUID STRAINER

If you use Bolink's Electro Whirl motor-cleaning fluid, you can filter it after use. Put a coffee filter paper into a jar, and pour the used fluid through it. *(Don't* pour the filtered fluid back into the container of unused fluid.) You can use the cleaning fluid two or three times.

PIVOT CLEAN-UP

To clean your car after a weekend of racing in dust, use a pipe cleaner to get grit out of the suspension pivots. Dip the pipe cleaner in alcohol to remove stubborn dirt.

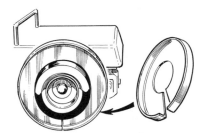

MOTOR SPLASH GUARD

If you hose down your wheels and tires, this simple splash guard will help to keep the electrics dry. Cut a large hole in the center of a butter-tub lid, split it as shown, and slip it over the suspension.

PORTABLE COMPRESSED AIR

For a quick clean-up, it's useful to have compressed air at the track. Carry an air tank and a 12V compressor that you can run off your auto battery. For safety, use a Sears or similar ASME-approved portable tank, and always wear some form of eye protection.

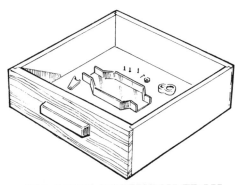

NO-LOSS ASSEMBLY TRAY

To prevent parts from getting lost, assemble your car in a drawer. No loose parts can bounce away, and when you want to stop working on the car, just slip the drawer back into the chest until next time!

SOLVENT-BATH PARTS HOLDER

Stainless-steel-mesh tea holders—the kind with a good latch and chain—are ideal for holding small parts like bearings. Suspend it in a closed container of solvent; dirt falls out, and the parts are kept clean.

MISCELLANEOUS

Certain tips belong in no specific category, but they still deserve a good look. This section contains useful advice that didn't quite fit anywhere else!

SECURING E-CLIPS

Sometimes, E-clips pop out of their grooves. To minimize the chance of this, smear clear silicone tub sealant over each clip, and when you want to remove one, the caulk will peel off easily.

BALL-JOINT SAFETY

Straight from aviation, here's a safety tip that prevents a ball joint from being totally disconnected if it pops loose. Put a washer on each side of the ball joint, making sure that the washers are slightly larger than the hole in the ball joint so that they can't pull through.

TRACK BARRIER

For clubs that are short of funds, lengths of 4-inch flexible-plastic drainpipe make an excellent, resilient, inside barrier for your track. These lightweight sections can be held together with duct tape, and they can be quickly taken apart and rolled up to fit into the car trunk.

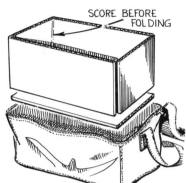

CARRYING CASE

Rather than spend a lot on a custom carrying case, pick up an inexpensive rectangular bag and line its sides, ends and bottom with heavy cardboard. You can use duct tape to keep it all together. Check your local TV store for those heavy tri-wall corrugated cardboard boxes, because they're ideal for this job.

HIGH-POWER SPOTLIGHTS

To modify the roll-bar lights on your Big Grizzly and *make them bright,* drill out the stud from the back of each light, then open the front piece. Sand around the edge of a Mini Mag flashlight reflector until it fits inside. Drill a small hole through which the wires can exit the lamp body, add a mini switch, and then hook it up to a battery.

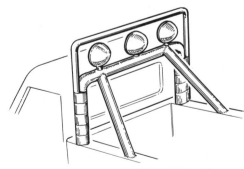

LIGHT PROTECTION—1

Most Blackfoot monster-truck lights seem to break off when the trucks roll over. To keep your Blackfoot lights in pristine condition, extend the roll bar to above the lights by taping a piece of hefty coathanger wire to the roll-bar uprights.

17 MISCELLANEOUS

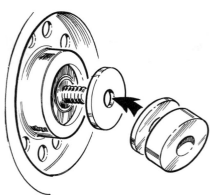

NYLON DIRT SEALS

If you replace your new vehicles' nylon wheel bushings with ball bearings, you can put the bushings to good use! Put a slice of bushing on top of each ball race before you add the retaining washer and nut. These nylon "washers" provide the bearings with an extra barrier against dirt.

METAL THREAD INSERTS

This works on the RC10 and the MRP GP-10. Where screws have to be threaded into plastic, dispense with the self-tapping screws and buy steel heli-coils at your hardware store. Install them according to the instructions. Now you'll be able to use machine screws, and you'll eliminate the problem of screws stripping out of the plastic, especially where components are regularly disassembled for cleaning.

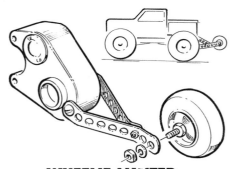

WHEELIE LIMITER

Does your Blackfoot do wheelies at the expense of the back bumper? If so, take a 4-inch and a 2½-inch length of Erector Set strip, and bolt them to the gear-case bolts, as shown. Then add a long bolt as an axle, and install a 1-inch-diameter model-plane wheel.

REPLACEMENT DRIVE PINS

Some common household nails fit well in the rear axle. Just cut them to length and file the ends smooth. For a tighter fit in the holes, put the nail on a hard surface (e.g., a table saw) then, using considerable pressure, roll the nail back and forth under the edge of a file to raise a slight knurl on it.

WHEELIE BARS

A Big Bear does nice wheelies—until you snap the bed off the body! To prevent this, cut these simple wheelie-bar brackets out of sheet metal, and bolt them to the motor. Using existing hardware, these bars can also be mounted on the CJ7 and the Toyota.

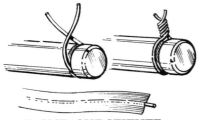

E-CLIP SUBSTITUTE

If you've lost your last spare E-clip, a bread-wrapper twist-tie is a good alternative. Wet the paper, then scrape it off the wire. The wire will fit nicely into the groove, where it should be wrapped around once and then twisted as shown.

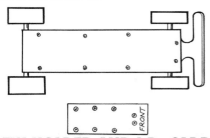

SCREW HOLDER AND I.D. CADDY

Usually, R/C cars use screws of several sizes, and when you disassemble a car, it's important to keep track of which screw goes where. This simple idea guarantees that you'll be able to put your car back together properly. Cut a piece of corrugated cardboard to the shape of your car, and mark the pattern of screw holes on it. As you remove each screw, put it into the corresponding hole in the cardboard.

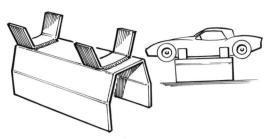

PVC CAR STAND

If you have a surplus piece of PVC gutter, you can make this very effective car stand. Assemble it with PVC pipe cement, silicone glue, or thick CA. You might need to line the U-shaped pieces with foam rubber or felt.

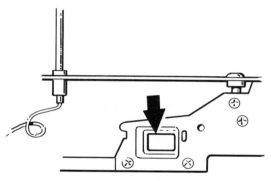

OPTIMA PUSH SWITCH

If you discard the regular switch and replace it with a suitable Radio Shack push-button switch that's installed where the resistor was originally mounted (arrowed), it's much easier to turn the car on and off.

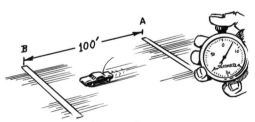

SPEED TRAP

Want to know the speed of your car? Make two highly visible lines across the track, about 100 feet apart. Station a stopwatch operator midway between them, then take a good long run at them for a "flying start." Start the watch as the car hits the first line, and stop it as it crosses the second one. Here's how to calculate your speed: 100 feet divided by the time taken (in seconds); then multiply the answer by 0.68 to arrive at mph.

$$\text{mph} = \text{distance covered (feet)} \div \text{time taken (seconds)} \times 0.68$$

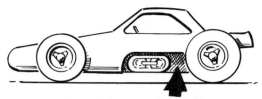

OPTIMA BATTERY ACCESS

If you cut away the sides of the car's body, you'll be able to swap batteries without having to remove it. This saves time, and you'll be less likely to lose body clips. This might work on other cars, too. Check yours.

MILK-JUG PARTS BIN

If you cut an empty milk jug as shown, it will hold all sorts of useful parts. (It's a great place to store spare tires). Laundry markers write well on the plastic, and if you label the jug just below its handle, it will be really convenient to lift off or put back on the shelf, with its I.D. readily visible.

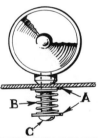

LIGHT PROTECTION—2

Here's a way to mount decorative lights on Lexan car bodies, or to mount lights so that they "give" on roll-over instead of snapping off. (The hood ornaments on most cars are mounted this way, too.) "A" is a washer, "B" is half of a ball-point-pen spring, and "C" is a thread-cutting screw. Tighten the screw to compress the spring

SHIPPING CASE

Going on a plane? Pack your car this way, and safely check the bag. Take an old suitcase and fill it with egg-crate foam sponge. Cut out slots for the wheels, so that the pan rests on the foam, then put foam blocks at both sides and both ends of the car. Next, cut out slots for your charger, parts and small tools.

ROLL-OVER PROTECTION

To protect your car from roll-over damage, as well as give it some self-righting capability, install twin, stiff, wire "antennas" on each side. Note the loops at the top of each for eye protection, and also note how the receiver antenna has been coiled around one of them.

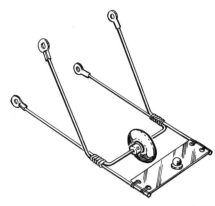

BIG BEAR WHEELIE-BAR/HITCH

This useful device is made of $1/8$-inch brass wire. Use a 1- to $1\frac{1}{2}$-inch-diameter airplane wheel, and center it with wheel collars. The brass hitch plate is also bound and soldered. Install a Kyosho ball joint, as shown.

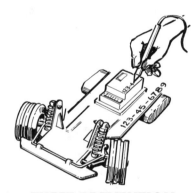

THEFT PREVENTION

Model cars and equipment are very portable—perhaps *too* portable for some light-fingered gentry. Engrave your Social-Security number on each chassis, receiver, battery pack, etc. This makes it tricky for thieves to dispose of equipment, and it certainly helps with identification if missing equipment is recovered.

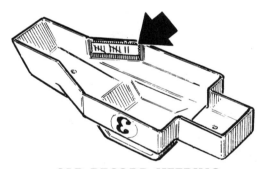

CAR RECORD KEEPING

Want to keep meticulous records? Put a strip of white tape inside your car's body, and record the number of runs made, etc., on it. You can also do this on your battery packs to record charge/discharge cycles.

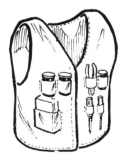

PIT VEST

Here's a useful garment for your pit manager! A photographer's vest can stow 33mm film cans containing nuts, bolts, etc. Better yet—modify the loops/pockets to hold spare tires and useful tools, as well as necessary screws.

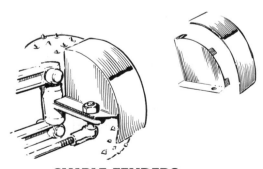

SIMPLE FENDERS

Are you fed up with the filth that sprays back from your front-wheel drive? Solder fenders made of thin tin plate, and bolt them to the steering arm, using the existing bolt. You could also cut out a section of a soft-drink can to serve the same purpose.

DUMMY CARS FOR CRUSHING
When this R/Cer ran his Clod Buster over perfectly good cars, he sometimes scuffed or damaged them. To prevent this, he nailed some old car bodies to suitable wooden supports. Now he has fun without damaging his cars or his pocket!

FAKING ACTION PHOTOS
Even if you don't own a camera with a high-speed shutter, you can still take action photos of your favorite car. Use a small twig to jack up the car, taking care to hide the twig in the shadow of a wheel or a tuft of grass. Have friend toss some dry dirt at the back of the car just before you press the button. This setup should help you create a convincing action shot. I did this with a full-size car once, and it worked beautifully.

MODELING CLAMP
A clothespin with its spring reversed gives you a clamp with deep jaws for that extra-long reach.

TRACTION COMPOUND APPLICATOR
Here's a way to avoid the usual mess you make when you apply traction compound to your car's tires. Remove the spring from a Bingo marker, wash out the ink, and fill the marker with compound. Replace the sponge cap, and you have a clean, easy-to-use applicator.

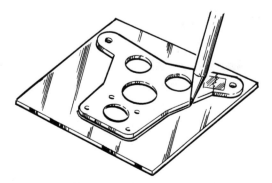

MAKING NEW SHOCK MOUNTS
To make replacement shock mounts, this car owner taped broken parts together, set them on a piece of 1/16-inch-thick aluminum and then traced the outline. Presumably, he cut them out with a fine-blade hacksaw, drilled the necessary holes and filed their edges. You can find aluminum at hardware stores or hobby shops.

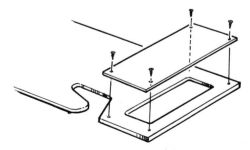

ROAD WIZARD STONE GUARD
Cleaning out the pebbles that get between the endbell and the motor mount is a chore. To eliminate this problem, make a Lexan cover for the opening that's below the motor in the T-plate, then secure the cover with four small sheet-metal screws.

R/C CAR ACTION BOOKS AND SPECIAL ISSUES!

BASICS OF RADIO CONTROL CARS
$9.95 (plus postage and handling)*

Your guide to the fun of R/C car modeling: *Basics of Radio Control Cars*, by Doug Pratt and the editors of *Radio Control Car Action*. The incredible growth in the popularity of R/C cars has created a need for an up-to-date book on R/C electric and gas cars. Learn everything you need to get started: building tips, modifications, batteries, motors, chargers, tools, finishing, R/C electronics and maintenance—they're all here! This book introduces the hobby and answers all your basic questions, but it can even teach experts a thing or two!

ADVANCED RADIO CONTROL CAR MODELING
$9.95 (plus postage and handling)*

From Rich Hemstreet and the editors of *Radio Control Car Action* comes the most up-to-date, informative book on R/C car modeling and racing. This book for advanced modelers covers the entire spectrum of R/C cars—everything from 1/24 to 1/4 scale, plus the new 1/10-scale stock cars. You'll find information on racing strategy, modifications, handling, gearing, tires, R/C electronics, 2-stroke engines, airbrushing Lexan and much more. What a wealth of information!—even the answers to many of your most difficult questions. Don't be left behind in the R/C race! Advance to our *Advanced Radio Control Car Modeling* book!

BASICS OF RADIO CONTROL BOAT MODELING
$9.95 (plus postage and handling)*

From John Finch and the editors of *Radio Control Boat Modeler* comes the number one book on R/C boat modeling and racing. *Basics of Radio Control Boat Modeling* gets you churning up the water. Power boats, deep-vees, hydros, monos, tunnels, in both gas and the new hot electrics—they're all here! You'll find in-depth info on R/C electronics, wiring, servos, batteries, 2-stroke engines, cooling systems, carburetors, speed controllers, hull nomenclature, drive systems, propellers, hardware setups, stuffing boxes, struts and bearings, trimming, balancing, timing, racing classes and a tremendous wealth of useful modeling and racing tips! We don't just tell you how, we show you, too!—there are hundreds of photographs and many illustrations.

RADIO CONTROL CAR ACTION OFF-ROAD
$4.95 (plus postage and handling)*

The overwhelming demand for up-to-the-minute information on the popular off-road segment of the R/C car hobby prompted the publication of this *OFF-ROAD Special*. It features 14 hot reviews, including the Schumacher Cougar, RC10 Graphite, Kyosho Lazer and Traxxas Radicator. A bonus "Buyers' Guide" includes many never-before-seen products, and the *OFF-ROAD Special* contains informative articles on getting started in off-road, troubleshooting, suspension set-up, budget motors, traction action and much more. Hands down, this special is where the off-road action is, and you won't want to miss out!

RADIO CONTROL CAR ACTION BUYERS' GUIDE
$4.95 (plus postage and handling)*

The *Car Action Buyers' Guide* is the only product guide available for R/C car enthusiasts—with over 300 info-packed pages! It's jammed with information on the latest in R/C cars and monster trucks, racing trucks, motors, tools, paints, bodies, conversion kits, wheels and tires, chargers, stock cars, bodies, off-roaders, 1/4 scale, hopup parts, suspension components, decals and more! You can't afford to be without this valuable R/C guide!

RADIO CONTROL MONSTER & RACING TRUCKS
$4.95 (plus postage & handling) *

Monster and racing trucks are the hottest segments of R/C today. This Special issue includes reviews of the newest trucks, a tire and wheel roundup, suspension tips, plus articles on airbrushing, heavy-duty speed controllers, conversions and much more. As a bonus, there's a special "Buyers' Guide" section and a colossal Truck Shootout! It's the only truck source available, and it will make a great addition to your R/C library.

ORDER NOW! Complete and return the order form below.
Credit-card orders, call toll-free: 1-800-243-6685 (in CT, 203-834-2900)

- -

RADIO CONTROL CAR ACTION BOOKS AND SPECIAL ISSUES

Please send me the following:

__ Basics of Radio Control Car $9.95*

__ Advanced Radio Control Car Modeling $9.95*

__ Basics of Radio Control Boat Modeling $9.95*

__ Radio Control Car Action Off-Road $4.95*

__ Radio Control Car Action Buyers' Guide $4.95*

__ Radio Control Monster & Racing Trucks $4.95*

Amount enclosed $ _____

Charge my: _____ MC _____ VISA ___ AmEx

Card # _____

Expire date _____ / _____ Signature _____

Name _____

Address _____

City _____

State _____ Zip _____

POSTAGE AND HANDLING: in the **U.S.**, add $2.95 for first item; $1 for each additional item. **Foreign Surface Mail** (including Canada and Mexico), add $4 for first item; $2 for each additional item. **Airmail**, add $7 for first item; $3 for each additional item. Payment must be in U.S. funds drawn on a U.S. bank, or by international money order. Connecticut residents add 8% sales tax.

Air Age Mail-Order Service, 251 Danbury Road, Wilton Ct 06897

AWESOME R/C ACTION!

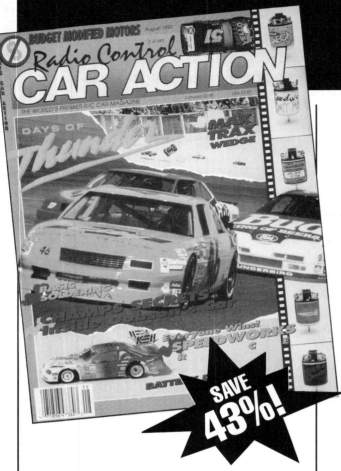

SAVE 43%!

You'll find it in *Radio Control Car Action!*

SUBSCRIBE NOW!

***Radio Control Car Action!* It brings you all the R/C action on wheels—**

It's jam-packed with R/C monster and racing trucks, off-roaders, stock cars, sports cars, gas- and electric-powered cars...you name it! *Radio Control Car Action* will put you at the front of the pack with hot R/C reviews, great "how to" articles, R/C electronics ideas, racing tips, radical modifications and more!

Subscribe now and save! Complete and return the order form below, or call toll-free: 1-800-435-0715
